THE UNITED ARAB EMIRATES

PROFILES · NATIONS OF THE CONTEMPORARY MIDDLE EAST
Bernard Reich and David E. Long,
Series Editors

ABOUT THE BOOK AND AUTHOR

This is the only study of the United Arab Emirates to provide an analytical treatment of the country and its people in their historical, social, economic, and political settings. Oil and strategic location confer upon the UAE an importance belonging to few other countries of its size, yet the attendant economic and security concerns can only be fully understood within a broad context of indigenous realities. This overview of the UAE begins with an extensive geographic-demographic description of the country and then examines its historical legacy, the sociocultural values of its people, economic development and prospects, and its domestic, regional, and international political concerns.

Since its creation in 1971 the UAE has defied pessimistic predictions of an early demise and has entered its second decade with strengthened prospects despite continuing uncertainties. The reasons for its survival and the obstacles it continues to face make its experience an instructive experiment in political federation. The UAE's extraordinary wealth, its tiny indigenous population, and its dependence on expatriate labor represent in an exaggerated way developmental issues that affect all the oil-rich countries.

Malcolm C. Peck is a program officer with Visitor Program Service of Meridian House International in Washington, D.C. He has served as the State Department's analyst for Arabian Peninsula affairs and as director of programs at the Middle East Institute. Peck holds a master's degree in Middle East studies from Harvard and a doctorate in international relations from the Fletcher School of Law and Diplomacy. He has contributed chapters to several books and written numerous articles on U.S. policy and interests in the Gulf–Arabian Peninsula area.

THE UNITED ARAB EMIRATES

A Venture in Unity

Malcolm C. Peck

Westview Press • Boulder, Colorado

Croom Helm • London and Sydney

Profiles/Nations of the Contemporary Middle East

Published in 1986 in the United States of America by Westview Press, Inc.; Frederick A. Praeger, Publisher; 5500 Central Avenue, Boulder, Colorado 80301

Library of Congress Cataloging in Publication Data
Peck, Malcolm C.
  The United Arab Emirates.
  (Profiles. Nations of the contemporary Middle East)
  Bibliography: p.
  Includes index.
  1. United Arab Emirates. I. Title. II. Series.
DS247.T8P42 1986   953'.57   86-1351
ISBN 0-86531-188-9

Published in 1986 in Great Britain by Croom Helm Ltd., Provident House, Burrell Row, Beckenham, Kent BR3 1AT

British Library Cataloguing in Publication Data
Peck, Malcolm C.
  The United Arab Emirates: A Venture in Unity.—
  (Profiles: Nations of the Contemporary Middle East)
  1. United Arab Emirates
  I. Title II. Series
    953'.053   DS247.T85
ISBN 0-7099-4038-6

Printed and bound in the United States of America

10   9   8   7   6   5   4   3   2   1

To my parents, Ruth and Wilfred Peck,
and to my wife, Aida, and son, John

Contents

ix

Tables and Illustrations

Acknowledgments

A book such as this owes a very great debt to many scholars and other specialists, as will be apparent in the footnotes and suggested readings. Dr. John Duke Anthony, doyen of U.S. scholars of the lower Gulf, has offered helpful advice and other assistance as have Dr. Edmund Ghareeb and Dr. Jasim Abdulghani. The wise counsel of the late Dr. Joseph J. Malone, as in many other enterprises, was of great value. Former State Department colleagues Kirk Augustine and Wayne White have kindly shared their reflections on developments in the Gulf–Arabian Peninsula area.

I am especially grateful to the Embassy of the United Arab Emirates in Washington, D.C., and the Ministry of Information in Abu Dhabi for making possible a trip to the UAE. I should like to record special thanks to Ibrahim el-Abed, director of the UAE national news agency WAM, who effectively assisted in arranging interviews for me in the midst of his frenetically busy schedule. Philip A. Wolcott, Jr., public affairs officer at the U.S. Embassy in Abu Dhabi at the time of my visit, provided generous assistance and, with his wife, Betty, gracious hospitality. Because some prefer not to be mentioned and because others might egregiously be omitted, I thank in collective anonymity the many people throughout the Emirates who kindly consented to share information, ideas, and opinions with me.

A fellowship in the fall of 1983 at the Middle East Institute, for which I am especially grateful to the institute's president, the Honorable L. Dean Brown, and its executive director, Dr. Philip H. Stoddard, helped to advance the research and writing of the book. MEI's librarian, Ruth Baacke, provided cheerful assistance with my research. I am indebted to Michelle Picard who expertly prepared the maps. My father and brother kindly made available their firm's computer graphics department to produce some of the charts. Ursula Nebiker magically transformed my rough manuscript into well-ordered electronic impulses.

I am especially appreciative of the forebearance of my editors, Dr. David E. Long and Professor Bernard Reich, and the publisher. Their patience, as the press of other obligations caused me to miss successive deadlines, was more than any author has a right to expect.

Finally, because most of the research and writing had to be done on evenings and weekends, a heavy burden was imposed on the rest of the family. I am, therefore, particularly indebted to my wife, Aida, for her constant support. My sister-in-law Consolacion, in the Filipino *bayanihan* (cooperation) spirit, helped to run the household while I scribbled. To my parents, Ruth and Wilfred Peck, I owe a debt of gratitude beyond repaying for their unfailing support and encouragement through the years.

Despite the assistance of the above and others, errors and shortcomings will undoubtedly be found. For these I assume responsibility with as much good grace as possible.

Malcolm C. Peck

Gulf–Arabian Peninsula region

Introduction

The United Arab Emirates (UAE), in successful defiance of the numerous predictions of failure made at its birth in 1971, has successfully completed a decade and a half as an independent federal state made up of seven semiautonomous emirates: Abu Dhabi, Dubai, Ras al-Khaimah, Umm al-Qaiwain, Sharjah, Fujairah, and Ajman. Moreover, it appears to have good expectations of surviving and enjoying reasonable stability for at least some time to come. Such an achievement alone would draw little attention to a country about the size of Maine, with a population of more than 1 million people (of whom only about one-fifth are citizens), were it not for the importance that oil and strategic location confer on the UAE.

The UAE is a major oil exporter and a key member of the Organization of Petroleum Exporting Countries (OPEC) and the Organization of Arab Petroleum Exporting Countries (OAPEC). The country has close and extensive economic ties with the United States and with its principal allies: Japan and the Western European countries. The UAE's status as a major international investor and aid donor is also significant to the United States, and the United States is obviously concerned about the vulnerability of the UAE and its similarly wealthy and militarily weak neighbors in the strategically vital Gulf–Arabian Peninsula area. (The body of water north of the UAE is called the Persian Gulf or the Arabian Gulf by some sources but in this book is referred to as the Gulf.)

With the principal aims of providing a reasonably full profile of the UAE, in this book I will endeavor to place economic, political, and security issues in a meaningful context of indigenous realities. Thus, the first chapter provides a geographic/demographic description of the UAE; those that immediately follow examine the historical legacy and social/cultural values of its people. A bit of background information may be helpful to those unfamiliar with the UAE. Prior

1

to the creation of the United Arab Emirates as an independent federal state in 1971, the emirates (also called shaikhdoms—the terms are essentially interchangeable) were known as the Trucial States, so called because of the truces imposed by the British on these states in the early nineteenth century to end piracy. The trucial system refers to the provisions of the several treaties on which the truces were based and the enforcement of the treaties by the British.

I hope that this book will persuade readers that the UAE is of interest for reasons beyond its great wealth and its strategic position. Its oil has made possible a developmental transformation of the country, the rapidity of which has not been paralleled anywhere else. The UAE's development illustrates, as if under accelerated laboratory conditions, the process of infrastructural and economic change and the profound consequences that flow from it, challenging the basic stability and continuity of the society. Also—to an extent not matched elsewhere—the UAE has become dependent on expatriate labor in committing itself to rapid development. Thus, its experience serves to illustrate in bold relief the problems and challenges of the modernization process, in the Third World generally and in other oil-rich countries particularly.

As an experiment in political unity the UAE provides an instructive case study of interaction between integrative and disintegrative factors. Because it has thus far proved to be a happy exception to the rule of failure in other such experiments in the Arab world, the UAE's experience is worth studying. This book will examine the structure and dynamics of the union as well as the crucially important noninstitutional factors that continue to play a very key political role.

The UAE is, in turn, part of a larger venture in regional cooperation—the six-Gulf Cooperation Council (GCC). The GCC represents significant progress among neighboring states in surmounting many of the divisive issues among them. At the same time, it was able to come into existence only because of the Iran-Iraq war, which has from September 1980 absorbed the energies of those two dominant Gulf powers. The GCC's principal preoccupation has been a search for ways to cope with the threat of Khomeini's Iran, but it also has taken meaningful steps toward greater economic cooperation and coordination.

Although the GCC reflects the Gulf nations' determination to provide their own security and exclude outside powers from the area, its inadequacy, like that of its members individually, in meeting potential regional and international security challenges is apparent. Like its weak, wealthy neighbors, the UAE is and will remain very vulnerable to various external threats. In that context this book will focus attention on the crosscurrents of regional and international forces that affect the UAE.

U.S. business has a significant stake in commercial relations with the UAE. The U.S. business community and the U.S. government share a deep concern anout the UAE's continuing security and stability. Americans generally have an interest in the survival and well-being of an economically important, politically moderate, and strategically vital country. For these reasons as well as the considerable inherent fascination of the land and its people, the UAE deserves our informed attention.

1

Land and People

In its geographic and demographic characteristics the UAE is broadly similar to the other Arab countries of the Gulf. Like them it is extremely arid, is endowed with important oil resources, and has a small population. However, there are some features that set the UAE apart. Although small in size, especially by comparison with Saudi Arabia, it has a much more substantial hinterland than the Gulf's other shaikhdoms—Kuwait, Bahrain, and Qatar—and its terrain displays greater variety in its features. Like its neighbors, the UAE has a large foreign population; in its case, the native population is, in relative terms, the smallest of all these states. Moreover, because the UAE, in contrast to the other Gulf shaikhdoms, is made up of autonomous states with their own distincitve historical experiences, there are numerous regional differences—economic, social, and cultural.

The United Arab Emirates is located in the eastern part of the Arabian Peninsula, astride the Tropic of Cancer, between 22°50'N–26°N and 51°E–56°25'E. Its Gulf coastline of approximately 430 miles is more than 40 percent of the total on the Arab side of the Gulf. The UAE's territory bisects the territory of Oman south of the Musandam Peninsula, giving the UAE a coastline of about 60 miles on the Gulf of Oman. Thus, the country forms a land bridge between the two bodies of water, just south of the strategic Strait of Hormuz, that Oman commands from the tip of the peninsula. The UAE shares land borders with Saudi Arabia on the northwest, west, south, and southeast and with Oman on the southeast and northeast (see Map 1.1).

The UAE's borders—thus also its area—cannot be precisely determined because of remaining undemarcated frontiers, some still in dispute (boundary disputes are discussed in Chapters 2, 5, and 6). Although agreement has apparently been reached with Saudi Arabia on the border that it shares with the emirate of Abu Dhabi,

4

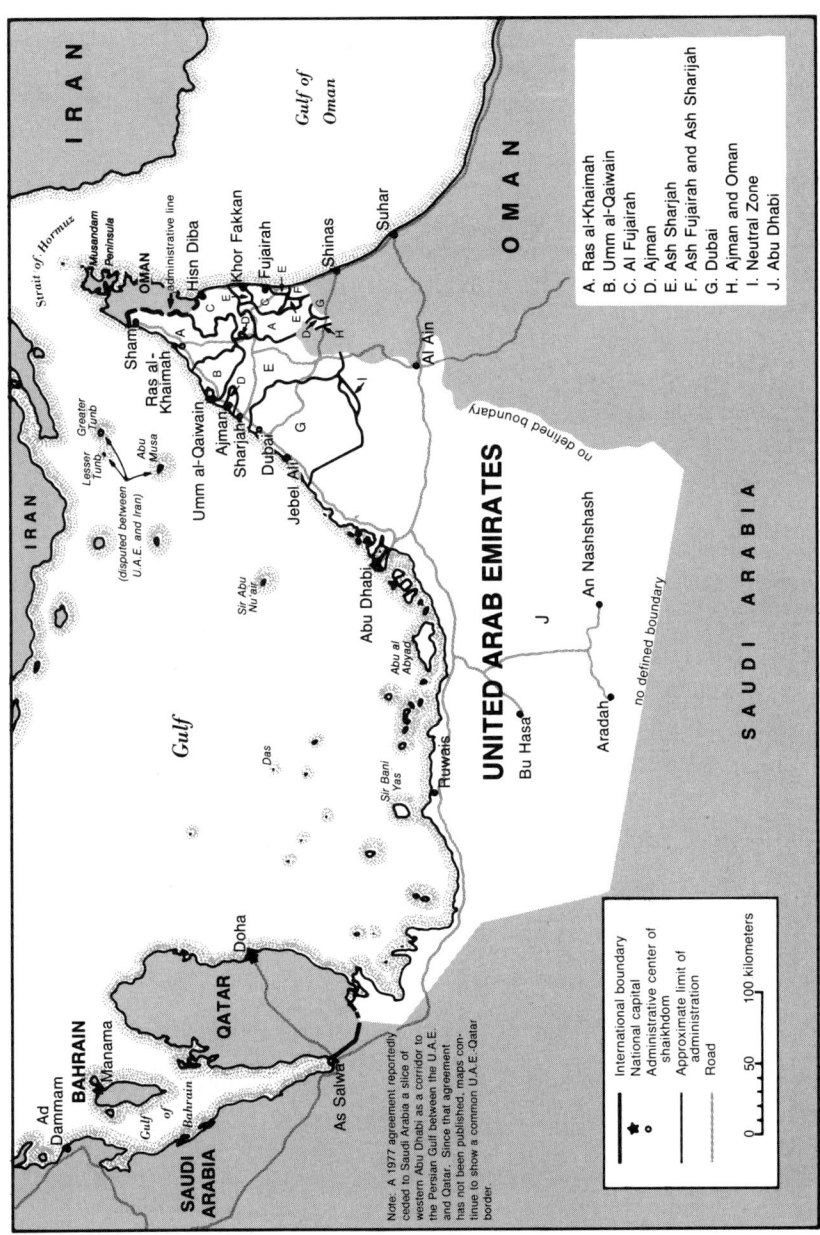

Note: A 1977 agreement reportedly ceded to Saudi Arabia a slice of western Abu Dhabi as a corridor to the Persian Gulf between the U.A.E. and Qatar. Since that agreement has not been published, maps continue to show a common U.A.E.-Qatar border.

A. Ras al-Khaimah
B. Umm al-Qaiwain
C. Al Fujairah
D. Ajman
E. Ash Sharjah
F. Ash Fujairah and Ash Sharjah
G. Dubai
H. Ajman and Oman
I. Neutral Zone
J. Abu Dhabi

International boundary
National capital
Administrative center of shaikhdom
Approximate limit of administration
Road

0   50   100 kilometers

MAP 1.1 Political boundaries of the United Arab Emirates and the lower Gulf

Table 1.1. The United Arab Emirates: Land Area

	(Square Miles)	(Square Kilometers)
Abu Dhabi	28,000	73,000
Dubai	1,500	3,900
Sharjah	1,000	2,600
Ras al-Khaimah	650	1,700
Fujairah	450	1,200
Umm al-Qaiwain	300	800
Ajman	150	400
TOTAL	32,050	83,300

Sources: The figures are based on those given in Richard F. Nyrop et al, eds., *Area Handbook for the Persian Gulf States* (Washington, DC: The American University for the US Government Printing Office, 1977), p. 300. The figures cited in Alvin J. Cottrell et al, eds., *The Persian Gulf States: A General Survey* (Baltimore and London: The Johns Hopkins University Press, 1980), p. 560, are generally close to the above, except that Abu Dhabi's area is represented as being somewhat smaller.

nonpublication of the terms of the agreement lends considerable uncertainty as to the UAE's western and southern boundaries. Estimates of Abu Dhabi's area, therefore, vary quite widely, and the figure used in Table 1.1 is consequently somewhat arbitrary. In addition, though most interemirate territorial disputes have been settled, the figures given for the areas of the other emirates cannot be considered as exact, though they provide a close approximation.

GEOGRAPHICAL REGIONS

The UAE may be broadly divided into four contrasting geographical regions: (1) the coast and the coastal plain into which it merges, (2) the interior desert, (3) the upland plains, and (4) the rugged mountains. A more picturesque style of division is the anatomical metaphor in which the mountains called *hajar* ("rock") divide the UAE into the *dhahira* ("back") and *batina* ("belly"), the broad Gulf and narrow Gulf of Oman littorals respectively. (Although the division between the upper and lower Gulf is somewhat inexact, Bahrain, Qatar, and the UAE are generally described as the states of the lower Gulf.)

The Coast and the Coastal Plain

Most of the long Gulf coast of the UAE, like virtually all the Arab littorals to the north, is an ill-defined junction of land and water, with numerous islands, reefs, and shoals and only one good natural harbor at Dubai (see Map 1.2). It is, thus, a difficult coast for navigation, and the very slight tilt of the Gulf floor creates off Abu Dhabi the shallowest part of the shallow Gulf. The light aquamarine tints that the casually observant air traveler will note extending well out into the Gulf translate on a bathymetric map into a 10-fathom line about 25 miles off the coast at Abu Dhabi city and more than 75 miles out from Qatar to the west. One consequence of this shallowness, combined with the extreme summer heat of the area, is that surface water temperatures along the Abu Dhabi coast may reach about 100°F, a temperature unsurpassed anywhere. Tidal currents are generally weak, except at the Strait of Hormuz, river estuaries, and narrow passages between land masses.[1]

Apart from a few geological peculiarities, the 250-mile coast of Abu Dhabi is without dramatic features. In the western part of Abu Dhabi the largest of the coastal salt flats, Sabkhat al-Matti, extends for more than 35 miles along the coast and for more than 60 inland. Under the summer sun, this and other sabkhas (Arabic *sibakh*), formed by the rising and evaporation of underground salt seepages, develop a hard crust on which vehicles can be driven. Rain or sea water, however, can either make a salt flat an impassable morass or weaken the surface crust so that it is extremely hazardous. The presence of sabkhas well above sea level is one of several pieces of evidence that the coast has been rising in recent geological times.

Farther east the coastline breaks into a series of islands, one of which is occupied by Abu Dhabi city. Toward Dubai the coast follows a flat, monotonous, and essentially unbroken course until the creek at Dubai, except for the new harbor west of Dubai at Jebel Ali. Sharjah commands an inlet, which though formerly silted up is now dredged and is, like Dubai's creek, a busy modern harbor. Urbanization has brought obvious and dramatic change to the coastal region of the UAE, with large and rapidly expanding cities existing where there were only modest settlements a generation ago. Indeed, with the contiguous urban area now represented by Dubai and Sharjah, expansion in Ajman and Umm al-Qaiwain may create a lower Gulf megalopolis of sorts stretching some 30 miles along the coast.[2] In 1948, Dubai, then the largest town in the Trucial States, had a population of 25,000. It is now a city of imposing skyscrapers and nearly 300,000 people that, bisected by a creek, presents a rather

8

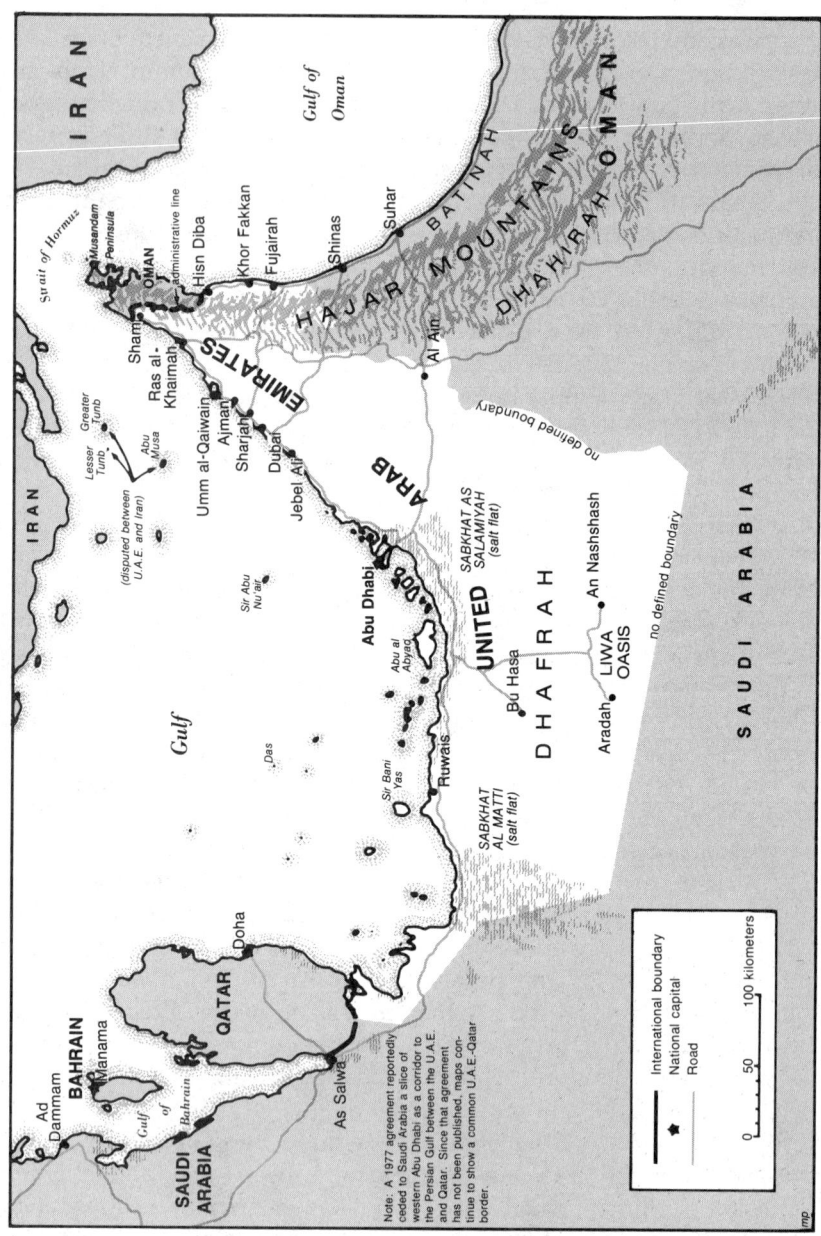

MAP 1.2 Physical features of the United Arab Emirates and the lower Gulf

The creek at Dubai. Dubai city is often referred to as the Venice of the Gulf. Its commerce, especially its role as an entrepôt, made it prosperous long before the emirate became an oil producer.

picturesque appearance, described by some as Venice on the Gulf. More striking still is the growth of Abu Dhabi from a small, nondescript town of about 2,000 in the late 1940s to an Arabian Houston with a population that approached 500,000 by the mid-1970s.

Dubai, with its sophisticated mercantile tradition and a history of urban planning dating back to the 1930s, has grown in an orderly if rapid manner. Under the ruler Shaikh Rashid bin Maktum's careful eye, it has retained its essential identity in a coherent and relatively graceful way. Abu Dhabi, by contrast, has until very recently expanded in a much less well-ordered fashion, reflecting to some extent its situation on a coastal island (with its irregular land mass) rather than along the clearly defined axis of a creek. Because Abu Dhabi also lacks Dubai's history of civic development, it has taken longer for a sense of coherent planning to be developed and imposed. Sharjah, in its physical development, has displayed something of an innovative spirit, two examples of which are its striking neotraditional *suq*, or market, and its introduction of pedestrian bridges over busy thoroughfares.

The cities of Ajman and Umm al-Qaiwain are located on less well-defined natural bays. It is only in the northernmost emirate of Ras al-Khaimah that the UAE's Gulf coastline assumes a dramatic character. Here, approaching Oman's Musandam Peninsula, the flat coastal plain gives way to cliffs, and rocky mountains reaching elevations of several thousand feet form a looming backdrop.

Desert shrubs and camel-thorn. In the area between desert and mountain just enough rainfall is received to support sparse vegetation on which camels and goats can forage.

The fairly wide coastal plain, an extension of the coast, extends from the western border of Abu Dhabi to Ras al-Khaimah, narrowing progressively from west to east. It essentially comprises a desert hinterland that bears little resemblance to any romantic visions of Arabian deserts. What one sees from the highway between Abu Dhabi and Dubai is typical of the coastal plain—an almost flat, nearly featureless sandy expanse of dull coloration with occasional unimposing dunes, camel-thorn scrub, and the rusting hulks of wrecked cars as the only visual distractions. In the northern emirates, however, where the coastal plain narrows between mountains and water, it displays rocky outcroppings with enough vegetation to appear lush by comparison with the land to the west.

The much shorter Gulf of Oman coastline is shared by enclaves of territory belonging to Sharjah and Fujairah, the latter being the only emirate with no Gulf coastline. Here the eastern slopes of the Hajar Mountains reach nearly to the sea, creating a setting of considerable scenic beauty. There are some pleasant beaches, and the water, in summer, is a few refreshing degrees cooler than on the Gulf side. A number of small settlements occupy narrow bits of coastal plain; where the plain widens sufficiently, there are larger settlements at Fujairah and Kalba. At Khor Fakkan there is a significant natural harbor.

The Desert

Inland from the immediate hinterland of Abu Dhabi's coast lies that part of the great Arabian desert that forms the northeasternmost extension of the Empty Quarter. A short drive along the new highway from Abu Dhabi city to al-Ain, the oasis settlement in the interior, carries one quickly into the desert. Just before entering al-Ain one passes a series of arrestingly beautiful dunes reaching a height of about 150 feet, hinting at the truly mountainous size of the dunes found beyond in the Empty Quarter. The dunes at al-Ain are tinged with iron oxide redness, but, with the changing light, undergo subtle alterations from pale rose to orange, thence to ocher, carmine, russet, umber and, in the last faint crepuscular glow of twilight, a deep purple. All across the sands the winds sculpt ever-changing patterns that with the permutations in coloring from both chemical composition and size of the grains endow the desert with a fascination that works its spell on the casual intruder in a four-wheel drive vehicle as it did on the great writer-explorers of earlier generations.[3]

Human settlement in this region, at least before the development of modern desalting technology, depended on the existence of sufficiently extensive aquifers at shallow depth either to provide oases where the water came naturally to the surface or to make possible the digging of wells. Al-Ain, a large circular oasis located about 100 miles east of Abu Dhabi city, is a classic example of the former phenomenon. Ten village settlements have grown up in the oasis, seven in Abu Dhabi and the other three across the border in Oman. (The oasis is also known as Buraimi after the name of one of the Omani villages.) Water for agriculture is drawn not only from open pits and wells but from a system of traditional underground tunnels, or *aflaj* (sing. *falaj*), that bring runoff water from the nearby mountains to al-Ain. Rapid population growth in the oasis is transforming the villages into a small city and is beginning to impose excessive demands on the oasis' natural water resources. A supplementary water supply is now piped from Abu Dhabi to al-Ain to meet rising demands and avoid damage to the aquifers.

The Abu Dhabi Department of Agriculture, following its creation in 1967, began its first project at al-Ain that same year. In the next year an experimental farm was established to determine what varieties of plants were best suited to local conditions and to promote their development. In 1974 an experimental farm also was established at Rawaya in Dubai.

Al-Liwa Oasis, as far to the southwest of Abu Dhabi city as al-Ain is to the east, is actually a series of some thirty oases spread in an arc forty miles from west to east. Good soil makes agriculture possible as at al-Ain, but cultivation is largely confined to the growing of date palms.

The settlement that has grown into Abu Dhabi city was established more than two centuries ago by the principal tribal group in Abu Dhabi, the Al Bu Falah, when fresh water was discovered on the island that the city occupies. Long before that, important coastal settlements had been established in Ras al-Khaimah because of the abundance of wells there. The existence of several aquifers not far below the desert's surface and the apparent subsidence of the water table as the land has risen reinforce other evidence of this area's past fertility. Recent archaeological discoveries of early settlements of culturally advanced people suggest that a far more extensive cover of vegetation existed in earlier historical times.

The Upland Plains

The gravel plains to the west of the Hajar Mountains on the Oman promontory as it narrows to the Musandam Peninsula form the third geographical zone in the emirates. Located mostly in Ras al-Khaimah and to some extent in eastern Sharjah, this is a much smaller but considerably more fertile region than either the coastal plain or interior desert. It represents the outwash from the foothills of the mountains, brought down through the wadis (Arabic *widayan*), or ravines; there are several areas in the gravel plains that support permanent natural vegetation and where at least limited agriculture is possible.

Several generally connected, semifertile plains extend from Jebel Sumaini in the south approximately 60 miles to the vicinity of Ras al-Khaimah town in the north, becoming progressively smaller from south to north. The southern area of Madam, located 30 miles north of al-Ain, has some woodland as does the plain of Dhaid above it. Further north the Jiri Plain has moderate vegetation, as does Sir, the northernmost area. Palm groves, acacia and eucalyptus trees, and some vegetables are grown in these areas. Camels and goats are also raised there.

Although only 5 percent of the UAE's territory is arable, Ras al-Khaimah's greater rainfall and the groundwater from the Hajar Mountains' runoff permit cultivation of 15 percent of that shaikdom's area. Half of the country's fruit, vegetables, cereals, and livestock is produced in Ras al-Khaimah, with dates, cucumbers, and alfalfa among the main crops.

The Mountains

The fourth distinct geographic zone in the UAE is the Hajar Mountains. The range begins to the southeast in Oman where the

Highway through the Hajar Mountains. Until the construction of roads to accommodate motor vehicles, the mountains and their fierce tribesmen constituted a barrier to movement between the two coasts of the UAE.

highest peaks are found. In the UAE their greatest elevation is about 5,000 feet, but the ruggedly dramatic character of these craggy masses gives them a much more imposing appearance than height alone would suggest. Some of the wadis in the mountains retain sufficient water to support modest agriculture. Dangerous flash floods can occur with the runoff of rainwater from the mountains down narrow ravines.

Until the advent of modern roads, these difficult mountains presented a considerable barrier to land travel between the Batinah coast and the emirates to the west. Local tribesmen frequently attacked outsiders who ventured there. By 1960 the security provided by the British-officered Trucial Oman Scouts (TOS) helped make feasible the construction of a road for motor vehicles to Fujairah through the Wadi Hamm. Today the Gulf of Oman coast is reached effortlessly on smooth, faultlessly engineered highways from several directions.

FLORA AND FAUNA

The UAE lies within a zone characterized by few species of flora. Some reference has been made to food crops and trees, both rainfed and irrigated; more is provided in the section on agriculture in Chapter 4. Here it may be mentioned that trees include irrigated stands of eucalyptus, acacias that are both rainfed and irrigated, and palms found in oases. Tamarisks and tamarinds grow naturally inland, and mangroves occur in swampy areas along the coast. A variety of hardy grasses and shrubs, among the latter the wild castor oil plant, manages to survive. Desert plants reveal a remarkable capacity to adapt to a harsh climate, and a rain following months or even years of aridity will bring to life a profusion of greenery and blossoms.

Similarly, a remarkably diverse representation of wildlife, in addition to the already noted domesticated animals, has adapted itself to a seemingly unpromising environment. Dozens of varieties of birds are present, either permanently or as migrants. Among these are hawks, gulls, and the Indian roller, a bird of dull brown outer plumage that reveals in flight brilliant, iridescent blue feathers. Falconry, the sport of desert shaikhs, is pursued in quest of the bustard, a tasty desert game bird. The waters of the Gulf support more than 200 species of fish, most of them edible, and among these are snapper, tuna, and the delicious hamour. In addition, there are several kinds of crustaceans, sea turtles, and the dugong, or sea cow.[4] Unhappily, the dugong and other surface-breathing marine animals may not survive the effects of the oil slick caused by leaking wells in the northern Gulf, another fallout of the Iran-Iraq war. Most of the more popular desert game animals have succumbed to modern carbines (even machine guns) and high speed motor vehicles. Efforts, however, have been launched to rescue the oryx, gazelle, and others from threatened extinction. Abu Dhabi's ruler, UAE President Shaikh Zayed bin Sultan al-Nuhayyan has made special efforts to prevent the killing of remaining specimens and to promote reconstitution of herds in protected areas. Shaikh Zayed is also responsible for the remarkable zoo at al-Ain. In 1969 he invited Johann Bulart, an Austrian civil engineer and amateur zoologist who had come to work for Shaikh Rashid in Dubai, to establish a facility, which was opened to the public the following year. Here animal species from around the world are represented, but local varieties are also featured; part of the zoo's new aquarium is devoted to the display of marine life from the Gulf.

CLIMATE

The seasons are essentially two: winter and summer. The former, extending from November through April, is generally pleasant, with temperatures mild enough for year-round swimming, i.e, between 68° and 95° Fahrenheit at midday. Evening temperatures at that time of year may dip as low as 48° Fahrenheit.

Winter is the season in which the UAE receives its scanty rainfall, although rainfall varies considerably in different parts of the Emirates

and even more from year to year. Between the winter seasons 1966–
1967 and 1974–1975 Abu Dhabi received an average of 1.7 inches
of rainfall annually, but the amounts ranged from .1 inches to 3.6
inches.[5] At Sharjah, where continuous observations have been made
since 1950, average precipitation is about twice what it is at Abu
Dhabi but with similarly great variation from one year to the next.
At the Agricultural Trials Station at Digdaga in Ras al-Khaimah,
rainfall is significantly greater than in Sharjah, with an annual mean
of 5.10 inches, although an average rainfall of 3.80 inches was measured
between 1959-1960 and 1965-1966.[6] To put these figures in perspective,
the average annual rainfall in Washington, D.C., not an unusually
wet locale, is 42 inches.

Summers, on the other hand, which extend from May to October,
have earned a just notoriety for their extreme discomfort. In the dry
desert interior, midday temperatures in the hot season are commonly
120° Fahrenheit or more. Along the coast average mid-summer highs
are a few degrees cooler but, accompanied by an oppressively high
humidity, make the worst August days in Washington, D.C., benign
by comparison. A fairly steady offshore breeze assuages the harshness
of the summer climate, but only slightly.

Along the lower Gulf coast evenings bring little if any relief
from daytime discomfort. The humidity intensifies, and the temperature
drops only a few degrees at dusk. The traveler arriving day or night
will experience a moment of breathless shock upon leaving a jetliner's
cool comfort and confronting the steambath-like atmosphere outside.
A short evening stroll from one's hotel will bring immediate, damp,
and rumpled defeat to even the most sensible, Western-style warm
weather clothing.

Before the introduction of modern air-cooling systems to the
UAE, wind towers, an Iranian invention, were the main source of
cool air circulation. Though once prevalent in buildings of premodern
construction, wind towers have all but disappeared (except where
replicated in the traditional Sharjah *suq*) and have been replaced by
air-conditioning. In few parts of the world has modern air-conditioning
so transformed the physical environment in which people must live
and work. All hotels, government offices, and commercial establishments of any consequence as well as all but the poorest immigrant
labor housing are air-conditioned. It is hard to imagine an urban,
modernizing society such as the UAE being able to function at a
reasonable level of energy and efficiency without modern air-conditioning.

At the same time, the products of modern technology suffer
considerably in the lower Gulf. Contemporary steel and concrete

Traditional UAE wind tower. This early form of air conditioning originated in Iran and helped to alleviate the severity of the lower Gulf's summer heat before the advent of modern cooling systems. The openings catch available breezes, and louvers direct the air downward, not actually lowering the temperature but creating a cooling effect. (Photograph courtesy of U.S. Department of State)

architecture does not fare well, acquiring a shabby appearance after only a few years of exposure to the hot, humid salt air. Corrosion similarly attacks motor vehicles and greatly shortens their average life.

As in other desert environments, sandstorms are a significant feature of the climate. They cause considerable damage to many manmade objects, especially those made of metal and glass, such as automobiles, and the sandstorms represent a travel hazard. Sandstorms in particular are associated with the *shamal*, a powerful wind from the north or west, and the hot *khamsin* from the south in summer. In the past the regular winds associated with the Indian Ocean monsoons were used to carry sailing vessels of the Gulf to India or Africa during one season and back during another when the prevailing winds reversed.

Some longtime residents of the emirates claim that the climate has moderated, with more temperate summers than previously. But has there really been a change in the climate? A report by the U.N.'s Food and Agriculture Organization (FAO) suggests a drop of some 4 or 5 degrees in summer temperatures; greater numbers of migrant birds and insects are presumed evidence of milder weather. In February-March 1982 phenomenal rains fell on the UAE. Records for a twenty-four-hour rainfall, the longest sustained rainfall, and the greatest amount of rain in a month anywhere on the Gulf coast were recorded. In a month's time more rain fell than had fallen in the more than ten years since independence, and the severely depleted aquifers of the UAE were fully replenished.[7] This was most probably an anomaly, unlikely to be repeated. In order to determine whether a meaningful change in UAE's climate has occurred, a longer period of weather observation is undoubtedly required.

POPULATION

The two most immediately striking features about the UAE's population are its rapid growth and the fact that resident foreigners greatly outnumber natives. Both circumstances are an outgrowth of the massive, extremely rapid modernization that followed discovery and production of oil in the 1960s and, especially, the oil price rises of 1973 and 1974.

In 1968 a census of the then Trucial States showed a total population of 180,226. By 1975 the population of the UAE was 655,937, an astounding 364 percent increase in seven years. By 1979 the population had reached an estimated 900,000 and stood at an estimated 1,130,000 as of 1982. Thus, though the rate of increase had slowed, the UAE's population continued to expand at a 12 percent annual growth rate between 1979 and 1982; in fourteen years it increased more than sixfold. However, the economic slump brought on by declining oil revenues has, as of the mid-1980s, caused a net outflow of expatriate workers and dependents. It is possible that the result will be a reduction of the total population by as many as 200,000 people. When this is combined with the rapid rate of natural increase among UAE citizens, it means that the trend by which UAE citizens had been reduced to a small minority in their own country has been significantly reversed.

The 1975 population was distributed by emirate as follows:

Abu Dhabi	235,662
Dubai	206,861
Sharjah	88,188
Ras al-Khaimah	57,282
Fujairah	26,498
Ajman	21,566
Umm al-Qaiwain	16,879

The same relative breakdown may be assumed at the present time but with somewhat more rapid growth in the oil-rich emirates of Abu Dhabi, Dubai, and Sharjah.[8]

The rate of natural increase for the native population is a high 2.5 percent annually. This is close to the annual net birth rates of 2.8 percent for Saudi Arabia and 2.7 percent for Egypt. By contrast, the rate of natural increase in the United States is insufficient to maintain the current population (only immigration has caused the modest growth rate of 4.7 percent during the 1980–1985 period). However, for the UAE it was the far higher rate of growth through immigration that overwhelmingly accounted for the vast population growth of recent years. Of the 180,226 residents in 1968, some 111,000 (about three-fifths) were citizens. Today UAE citizens make up only one-fifth of the total population. Because 80 percent of the UAE's inhabitants are there in response to the country's need for diverse job skills (counting both workers and the dependents that accompany a minority of them), the immigrants give the population a very diverse complexion and a distinctly youthful and male character.

Several South Asian groups together make up about one-half the total population. In 1980 both Indians and Pakistanis outnumbered the native population by 23.5 percent and 20.2 percent respectively. Non-UAE Arabs of various nationalities accounted for just under 15 percent of the UAE's population, with Omanis, Palestinians, Jordanians, Egyptians, and Yemenis most heavily represented. Europeans, East and Southeast Asians, and U.S. citizens, collectively, were slightly more than 5 percent. One source claimed that Iranians represent more than 16 percent of the total population. Although that estimate may be high, the actual figure is still considerable.[9] This diverse population is found mainly in the urban areas of the three wealthy emirates—Abu Dhabi, Dubai, and Sharjah, and overwhelmingly in the first two. This heterogeneity has long characterized Dubai, with its history as an entrepôt, but not Abu Dhabi. In 1948 the British author Wilfred Thesiger wrote of Dubai: "The *suqs* were crowded with many races—pallid Arab townsmen; armed Bedu, quick-eyed and imperious; Negro slaves; Baluchis, Persians, and Indians. Among them I noticed a group of Kashgai tribesmen . . . and some Somalis."[10] However, in the poorer northern emirates, to the present, the immigrant population has remained much smaller.

The high rate of natural increase for UAE nationals—a result of cultural preference for large families and improved health standards—and the fact that most expatriates are workers between the ages of 20 and 40 means that both natives and immigrants are very young. They can, at the same time, expect to live much longer than earlier generations because current life expectancy, reflecting the impact of modern health care, is 62.4 years.

Because most immigrant workers are men and because restrictions against accompanying dependents have been implemented in recent years in response to the huge increase in the expatriate population, more than 70 percent of the total population is male. Some of the economic, political, social, and cultural implications of the presence of the exceedingly large expatriate population and its multi-skewed nature are examined in Chapters 3 and 5.

The UAE's population is predominantly urban. The three largest cities—Abu Dhabi, Dubai, and Sharjah—account for about 80 percent of the UAE's population. Larger towns such as al-Ain, Ras al-Khaimah, Fujairah, Ajman, Umm al-Qaiwain, Kalba, Khor Fakkan, Dibba, and Dhaid account for the greatest part of the remaining 20 percent. With the creation of new cities at Jebel Ali in the emirate of Dubai and Ruwais in Abu Dhabi, the urbanization of the country's population is even more pronounced. One source gave the UAE urban population as 84 percent of the total in 1980.[11]

NOTES

1. Alvin J. Cottrell et al., eds., *The Persian Gulf States: A General Survey* (Baltimore and London: Johns Hopkins University Press, 1980), pp. 541–542.

2. See Michael E. Bonine, "The Urbanization of the Persian Gulf Nations," in Cottrell, *Persian Gulf States*, p. 265.

3. Of special interest in this regard is Wilfred Thesiger's *Arabian Sands* (New York: Penguin, 1980). Thesiger twice crossed the Empty Quarter by camel, the second time continuing across Abu Dhabi to the oases of al-Liwa and al-Ain.

4. See the appendixes "Flora" and "Fauna" in Cottrell, *Persian Gulf States*, especially pp. 575, 578–579.

5. See K. G. Fenelon, *The United Arab Emirates: An Economic and Social Survey*, 2d ed. (London and New York: Longman, 1976), table on p. 136.

6. Donald Hawley, *The Trucial States* (London: George Allen and Unwin Ltd., 1970), p. 179.

7. See Trevor Mostyn, ed., *The UAE: A MEED Practical Guide* (London: Middle East Economic Digest Ltd., 1982), p. 144, and Department of State, "The Greening of the United Arab Emirates," airgram, U.S. Embassy in Abu Dhabi, March 23, 1982, p. 10.

8. The figures are drawn from Fenelon, *Economic and Social Survey*, p. 598 and from the "Department of State Background Notes," on the UAE for 1982.

9. *UAE MEED Special Report* (November 1984):76.

10. Thesiger, *Arabian Sands*, p. 276.

11. See Paul Barker, "Boom Towns of the Gulf: The Rush to Service the Cities," in *8 Days* (London), June 6, 1981.

2

The Historical Background

The history of the United Arab Emirates as a nation only began in 1971, and the land it occupies was not generally considered important prior to the discovery of oil. In the past, however, this land was one of the earliest seats of civilization in the Middle East. The ancient history of what is now the UAE, and of the Gulf as a whole, remains largely conjectural. What is clear is that a highly developed civilization existed here even before ancient Egypt's first united kingdom came into being and that after a millenium this civilization disappeared.

Only in the last few years has this rich and fascinating past of the Arab side of the Gulf come to light. The absence of precise references in known historical documents and the remoteness of the area from earlier archaeological explorations preserved its secrets. Moreover, a conservative Muslim indifference or active hostility toward investigation into the pre-Islamic past, or "age of ignorance," though not a part of orthodox Islamic doctrine, has until the present impeded serious investigation of those ancient sites in the Arabian Peninsula that were known. Now, however, Arab as well as European and U.S. scholars are enthusiastically involved in the work of revealing the UAE's ancient past.

The discovery process began with a Danish archaeological expedition from the Aarhus Museum of Prehistory to Bahrain in 1953.[1] The Danish scholars' investigation of the burial mounds of Bahrain and the culture that produced them soon revealed that an advanced trading civilization, dating back to the early third millenium B.C., had existed on the island. This culture was linked both to the ancient Sumerian culture of the Tigris-Euphrates Valley to the north and to the Indus civilization of that time centered on Mohenjo-Daro. The Danish archaeologists decided that the evidence was sufficient to establish the site excavated on Bahrain Island as Dilmun, a fabled

21

kingdom mentioned in Sumerian texts and a leading candidate as the site of the Garden of Eden. Even though not all scholars agreed that Bahrain was the location of Dilmun, what is clear is that the Bahrain culture was part of a network of ancient trading settlements along the Arab side of the Gulf.[2]

The Danish expedition's attention turned to Abu Dhabi when Temple (Tim) Hillyard, a British Petroleum employee and amateur archaeologist, reported the existence of tumuli (mounds), apparently like those on Bahrain, on Umm al-Nar, a small island just east of Abu Dhabi city.[3] (In eastern Arabia much valuable preliminary archaeological exploration has been carried out by weekend amateur enthusiasts who are employees of oil companies like Aramco or other corporations operating there.) When the same Danish scholars began digging at the Umm al-Nar site in 1959, it marked the first scholarly archaeological work to be carried out in the UAE (then the Trucial States). The antiquity of the culture was soon apparent, but only after six years of investigation was it unexpectedly discovered that Dilmun (or what was believed to be Dilmun) and Umm al-Nar were part of the same culture. As long ago as 2800 B.C. they were components of a Gulf civilization engaged, like their counterparts today, in trading across the known world.

In 1960 Shaikh Zayed, now ruler of Abu Dhabi and president of the UAE, then governor of al-Ain, invited the archaeologists to explore tumuli on the edge of neighboring Jebel Hafit, a mountain south of al-Ain. In subsequent years this and other nearby sites were explored, and stone implements dating as far back as 5000 B.C. were discovered. At Hili, a village in al-Ain Oasis, evidence of an extensive, prosperous community was found. This evidence included stone relief carvings of impressive quality on tombs. One that depicted a love-making couple recalled similar representations in Indian art but was, as the leader of the Danish expedition Dr. Geoffrey Bibby remarked, with his tongue in his cheek, "hardly the thing for grave-chamber decoration."[4]

Although archaeological expeditions may continue to yield long-buried secrets in the years to come, dramatic revelations about the early history of the land already have come to light, in particular the extraordinary transformation the climate has undergone since ancient times. Rainfall then was far greater than is now the case, and in the area of al-Ain some significant residue of former fertility remains. But at Umm al-Nar and the more recently discovered site of an ancient settlement at Khor al-Udaid, near Qatar, today's barren sands offer no hint of the relative lushness that made possible the existence of early civilizations. Presumably the onset of pronounced

The al-Ain Museum. The fort from which the Al Nuhayyan family ruled in al-Ain now houses a collection of artifacts drawn from archaeological digs in the vicinity; some artifacts date back nearly five thousand years.

desertification explains the disappearance of the ancient Abu Dhabi civilization after an existence of about one thousand years. Another intriguing discovery is the likelihood that the camel was first tamed in this area. It was known and eaten at Umm al-Nar one thousand years before its introduction farther north.

Fascinating questions remain. Were the ancient settlements discovered in Abu Dhabi connected with what Bibby calls the "second 'lost civilization' of the Lower Sea, the copper kingdom of Makan"?[5] Some scholars believe Makan (or Magan) to have been located somewhere in present-day Oman. Once archaeological investigations are carried out there, the connections between the various outposts of ancient culture on the Arab side of the Gulf may become more clear—or possibly new lines of inquiry will be raised.[6]

In addition to these places of legend whose stones have yet to be unearthed, other sites of varying antiquity have been found that add more pieces to the complex mosaic. For example, near the town of Dibba on the Gulf of Oman side of the UAE there is evidence of what appears to have been an extensive ancient settlement, but one presumably not connected with the Umm al-Nar culture. Not far from Dhaid in Sharjah a team of Iraqi archaeologists in 1972 and 1973 discovered an interesting site dating to Seleucid times. A year later the same team excavated part of al-Darbahaniyya, an important port in the later Islamic period. In 1981 Iraqi scholars unearthed a trading center of three thousand years ago in Dubai.[7] With the stimulation of enthusiastic Arab interest in the past and the continued growth of scholarly competence in archaeology, exciting discoveries in the UAE and neighboring countries are likely to continue, thereby reducing conjecture and increasing knowledge about their ancient past.

BETWEEN ANCIENT AND MODERN TIMES

Little evidence exists to illuminate the centuries between 1000 B.C. and A.D. 1600, when the history of the Gulf region first intersects that of Europe. One writer has identified these long centuries as a "historical void" in the background of the UAE.[8] Current and future archaeological research may fill in part of this vast gap. Indeed, restoration has begun on several recently excavated monuments in Ras al-Khaimah, among them a citadel used by the army of Alexander the Great on its way to invade India and reputedly the winter palace of Queen Zenobia of Palmyra.[9]

Along much of the Gulf coast and in nearly all the interior regions, tribal developments characterized by endless flux left little that modern researchers can draw on to reconstruct hundreds of years of the area's history. We do know that migrations of Arab tribes in the early centuries of the Christian era played an important role in populating the land, giving it, by Islamic times (early seventh century A.D.), an overwhelmingly Arab imprint. From the second century A.D. to the sixth, groups moved up the south Arabian coast to occupy much of the Hajar Mountain area and al-Ain Oasis (then called Tu'am or Tawwam). Later migrations from the north added to the Arab tribal mix of what is now the UAE.[10] We know more of developments generally in the broader Gulf region because, for most of the period in question, the region was under the domination of great empires, from east and west, that replaced the small, interlinked commercial states of the earlier era. This provides us with some sense of the larger context in which the Gulf and the peninsula were actors.

Although there are sketchy reports of the activities of Phoenicians, Assyrians, and Babylonians in the Gulf earlier in the first millenium B.C., the history of the region first acquires a more coherent character in the year 550 B.C. when Cyrus the Great founded the first Persian empire, the Achaemenid. This united the vast area constituting Western

Asia and Egypt and helped to promote a major trade between the Gulf and India.

Two centuries later the Achaemenid Empire fell before the Macedonian armies of Alexander the Great. Alexander had ambitious plans for developing the Gulf trade, east and west, from the new imperial capital he would build in Babylon. He proposed to capture the Arabian Peninsula and colonize its shores to promote his empire's maritime commerce. But, on the point of launching this expedition, Alexander died, and his successors in the eastern part of the empire, the Seleucids, never pursued these grandiose schemes. They only modestly developed the commercial possibilities of the Gulf.

For much of the Hellenistic and Roman periods the Gulf trade was in the hands of small, largely Arab towns. With the rise of the second great Persian empire, the Sasanid, in the early third century A.D., the Gulf trade received a great new impetus. Increasingly, merchant ships sailed all the way to China, which Arab mariners of the lower Gulf had long since reached, and for nearly one thousand years a great part of the Gulf's trade continued to flow along that route. However, in the lower Gulf the maritime activity of the Arabs suffered under the control of the Sasanids, who extended their direct rule to East and South Arabia (i.e., the eastern and southern areas of the Arabian Peninsula) by A.D. 600 and dominated trade.[11]

By the middle of the seventh century A.D. the Islamic conquests had swept away the Sasanid Empire. Eastern Arabia accepted Islam before the Prophet Muhammad's death in A.D. 632, subsequently lapsed into apostasy, and then was brought back forcefully into the fold. The decisive battle in recovering for Islam the area of historical Oman—the present day Sultanate of Oman and the UAE—was fought at Dibba on the Gulf of Oman side of the Emirates.[12] Southeast Arabia, remote from the centers of Islamic power in Mecca, Medina, Damascus, and Baghdad, was a stronghold of various heterodox movements, beginning with the populist, fanatical Kharijites in the late seventh century A.D. In the late ninth and tenth centuries a more extreme schism, the Qaramita (or Carmathians) swept Eastern Arabia and destroyed the Omani state of the Ibadis, yet another movement away from the mainstream of Islam. The Ibadis, of Kharajite origin but not far removed in belief and practice from Sunni, or orthodox, Islam, have remained entrenched in mountainous inner Oman to modern times.

Nevertheless, Islam had the effect of uniting Arabia for the first time and of bringing both coasts of the Gulf under Arab Muslim rule. This led to the period of greatest flowering of Gulf commerce with India and China, under both Arab and Persian merchants, from the seventh to the tenth centuries A.D. Indeed, as one contemporary sailor-author who sailed the route to China on a reconstructed traditional sailing vessel observed: "Arab merchants had established the most widespread sea-borne trading network the world had ever known, a network that was not to be matched for another seven hundred years when the globe was first circumnavigated by a European ship."[13] We know that Julfar, now the city of Ras al-Khaimah, was an important Gulf port in the mid-eighth century and, somewhat later, the terminal of a major trade route to what is now al-Ain. Arab seamen remained the leading traders of the Indian Ocean until the Portugese irruption into eastern waters in the sixteenth century, though the disruptive impact of the Carmathians in Arabia and an earlier destructive rebel revolt in China in A.D. 879 kept the China trade from again achieving its earlier peak.

The ships that accomplished the long voyages across the Indian Ocean and beyond the East Indies were rather frail but graceful, well-designed craft generally of teakwood planks from India, held together not by nails but by sewn coconut fibers. The preferred season for sailing from the Gulf was September or October when the ships could exit on the northeast monsoon. Because of delays in waiting for favoring winds to and from Canton, the China trade round trip required about eighteen months. The dangers of such a voyage were extreme, with high losses of ships. Even in the early twentieth century, one in every ten Arab ships sailing across the Indian Ocean was lost.[14]

These ships, to which the collective term *dhow* (a word of Swahili origin) became attached through British usage, were all double-ended and pointed at both ends, before European influence led to the construction of the squared-stern types. The "boom" in modern times (a large vessel with pointed bow and stern, rigging, and usually a motor) continued the earlier style of design. Other traditional Gulf ships, which were the principal craft of the Gulf through the first decades of the twentieth century, were distinguished by the size and shape of their hulls and known by the names *baggala, jalboot,* and *sambook.* Captain Alan Villiers, who sailed on these ships and recorded his adventures in *Sons of Sinbad,* rightly laments their passing.[15] However, some continue to ply the Gulf, fitted as motor-powered vessels, and in the UAE and elsewhere some traditional Gulf sailing ships again are being built for recreation and display.

The Portuguese Appearance in the Gulf

The Arab ships were no match for the Portuguese men-of-war that made their appearance in the Indian Ocean at the opening of the sixteenth century. The Portuguese aimed at monopolizing trade with the Indies by outflanking the traditional routes between Europe and the East—the Gulf and the Red Sea—using the route around the Cape of Good Hope that Portuguese navigators had discovered in the late fifteenth century. Animated also by a religious zeal that carried over from the centuries of Muslim-Christian conflict in the Iberian Peninsula (the Reconquista that had then just concluded), the Portuguese came as conquerors who sought to impose their rule in the Gulf, indeed throughout Asia.

Affonso de Albuquerque, the brilliant Portuguese military leader, saw the Strait of Hormuz as one of the key strategic positions whose possession would secure control of the vast Indian Ocean–East Indies region. His seizure of the island of Hormuz was key to a century of Portuguese control of the Gulf. One of the places that Albuquerque captured was Khor Fakkan, today an important container port on the Gulf of Oman coast in an enclave of the emirate of Sharjah and at that time a prosperous port with numerous wealthy Indian merchants.[16] In the mid-sixteenth century the Ottomans, then extending their imperial sway over the Arab world, confronted the Portuguese in the Gulf. By the late sixteenth century the latter's superior seamanship had overcome the Ottoman challenge. However, not long after repelling this threat, with their strength undercut by various factors including financial weakness and internal dissension, the Portuguese succumbed in the early seventeenth century to the superior naval forces of the Dutch and British. One of the last places where the Portuguese retained a foothold was Ras al-Khaimah. However, neither there nor in the other parts of the Gulf where they established themselves did the Portuguese leave a lasting legacy. Domineering, exploitative, and aggressively hostile to the Islamic culture of the Gulf's population, they barely disturbed the rhythm of the region's life and left its institutions intact. It would be another three centuries before the outside world would intrude sufficiently to bring basic changes to the economic, social, and political modes of Arab life in the lower Gulf.

British and Dutch Ascendance in the Gulf

The establishment of the English and the Dutch East India companies in 1600 and 1602 respectively foreshadowed the Portuguese eclipse in the Gulf. In 1622 the British assisted the Persians in recovering Hormuz from the Portuguese and three years later combined with the Dutch to defeat Portugal's attempt to regain its position there. For the rest of the century the two ascendant maritime powers vied for supremacy in the Gulf: The Dutch generally had the upper hand.

Throughout much of the eighteenth century control of the Gulf fluctuated, residing sometimes in the hands of outside powers and other times in those of local leaders. But insecurity was the general rule as the Safavid empire declined and local powers rose to take its place. This instability resulted in an increase in Gulf piracy in the latter part of the century—with Omanis playing the leading role, though joined by U.S. and English buccaneers, among others. The resulting disruption of commerce led the British East India Company to appeal to the Royal Navy to suppress piracy in the region. By the end of the eighteenth century the Dutch were in decline, and the French, pursuing Napoleon's eastward ambitions, were England's chief rival for control of the waters of the Gulf and the Indian Ocean. In 1798, the year of Napoleon's expedition to Egypt, the British East India Company reached an agreement with the Imam of Muscat that excluded the French from his territories, assented to the establishment of an armed British trading settlement at Bandar Abbas, and (two years later) allowed a British agent to reside at Muscat to conduct all business for England.[17] This set the stage for the British imperium in the Gulf that would endure for a century and a half.

The Rise of the Qawasim

British involvement in the Gulf might have remained confined entirely to commerce except for circumstances in the Oman–lower Gulf area that gave rise to an increase in piracy and severely menaced British interests after the French threat had dissipated. The British response also took place in the context of the rise of the Qawasim (singular, Qasimi). The Qasimi was the ruling clan. They and their followers were often referred to in British sources of the time as Joasmee, following local pronunciation. The ruling families of both Sharjah and Ras al-Khaimah today are Qawasim, descendants of the ruling shaikhs of two centuries ago. By the early nineteenth century Qasimi rule was consolidated along the Gulf coast north and east of Dubai and into the Musandam Peninsula. Qasimi ships dominated the waters of the lower Gulf and came increasingly into hostile contact with the British vessels and Britain's Indian subjects. The Qasimi federation also challenged Oman's maritime supremacy and the expansion of Saudi political/religious influence into the southeast quadrant of the Arabian Peninsula.

In the second and third decades of the eighteenth century Oman was torn by a civil war between two tribal factions, the Hinawi and the Ghafiri; these factions were part of a basic division among the peninsula tribes dating back to pre-Islamic times under the names Adnan and Qahtan. (This seemingly anachronistic source of identity preserves its relevance today: A tribesman in the UAE will know to which faction his tribe and most others in the area adhere.) One Omani faction invited the intervention of the Persians who soon became would-be occupiers, and the Persian intervention generated a degree of unity in Oman that was consolidated (apart from the Ibadi interior) under the Al Bu Said dynasty, which reigns today. The weakening of both Iran and Oman at this time opened the way to an assertion of Qasimi power.

The origins of the Qawasim are somewhat obscure. They were part of a migratory group of peninsula Arabs called Hawala (probably from the Arabic verb meaning "to move to a new residence") that left central Arabia to settle in Persia shortly after the Islamic conquest of that country in the mid-seventh century. Subsequently, the Hawala occupied both shores of the Gulf. The Qawasim forced the weakened Omanis to acknowledge Qasimi independence in northern Oman. (Historical Oman included the area now occupied by the UAE, though, to confuse matters further, the Gulf coast east of Qatar came within Arab geographers' definition of Bahrain at one time. What came to be called the Trucial States or, misleadingly, Trucial Oman, was known earlier as al-Shamal or al-Sir.) By the end of the eighteenth century the Qawasim were forcefully contesting Omani maritime primacy in the Gulf and in the Indian Ocean.[18] The Qawasim were made even more formidable opponents to the Omanis and a general menace to commerce by their alliance with the Saudi state's reformist Islamic power and fervor in the first decade of the nineteenth century, an alliance the Qawasim found politically useful. By 1800 a Saudi force had seized the Buraimi Oasis, which served as a base of operations against Oman for the next eighteen years.

The Qawasim-Wahhabi Alliance

A mixture of proselytizing zeal and coercive force brought several tribes to the side of the Wahhabis. (Muhammad ibn Abdul Wahhab launched a conservative Islamic reform movement in the mid-eighteenth century, which has provided to this day the legitimacy of the Al Saud, rulers of Saudi Arabia. His followers were called Wahhabis by their detractors. They themselves rejected, as the Saudi followers of Abdul Wahhab's teachings do today, any term that suggested any deviation or derogation from pure Islam. They called themselves "unitarians," emphasizing the centrality of God's unqualified oneness in Sunni Islam.) The Qawasim, already inclined to simple Sunni orthodoxy and eager for a powerful ally against their Omani enemies, allied themselves readily with the new reformist power. This both strengthened them against the Omanis and added a frightening tinge of fanaticism to their depradations on the high seas, which included the slaughter of the crews of several captured vessels.

Different theories have been set forth to explain the upsurge in attacks on shipping in the Gulf and Indian Ocean, with the Qawasim in the lead, that occurred in the early nineteenth century. Arabs are inclined to describe as "maritime warfare" the attacks that were largely directed against other Arabs; the English of the time and most Westerners since have tended to see them as piracy. A distinguished retired British official with long service in the Gulf wrote that "under the guise of religion, the pirates slaughtered all captives whose religious views did not coincide with theirs." In contrast, a contemporary Arab scholar suggested that the term "piracy" more properly describes the European naval action against the Arabs than the activities of the latter.[19]

The semantic quarrels are interesting principally as reflections of a clash between cultures, but a search for causes, by whatever name, is more to the point. Pirates had been known in the Gulf from earliest historical times and by the eighteenth century included celebrated English and U.S. representatives. The relative poverty of the population along the Gulf shores had always turned many indigenous seafarers to at least part-time practice of piracy. As one scholar observed, the outburst of widespread maritime violence in the early nineteenth century probably resulted from a general attempt by numerous Gulf seamen, but principally the Qawasim, to seize a larger share of the trade that Oman had dominated.[20] Another writer has pointed out that had it not been for the subsequent British intervention, the Qawasim could have commanded most of the Gulf's trade, suggesting that they were more interested in extending their control over that commerce than in piracy per se.[21]

Piracy in the Gulf and the British Response

British interest in the Gulf had, from the beginning, been commercial rather than strategic and remained so after 1800. Thus, the British government in India, which was responsible for British policy in the Gulf, was slow to take action in protecting British and Indian shipping against attack. One British writer on the Gulf disgustedly observed that "the height of audacity reached by these Joasmee ruffians" was due largely to the "wavering and infatuated policy of the Bombay Government . . . in regarding the pirates as 'innocent and unoffending Arabs'—to use the Governor's own words."[22] British expeditions in alliance with Omani forces in 1806, 1809, and 1816 only temporarily checked the Qawasim marauders, and by 1817 the Qawasim were spreading terror along the Indian coast to within 70 miles of Bombay.[23] This helped to generate a major British expedition in 1819, which defeated the Qawasim.

The Qawasim naval confederation, centered on the port of Ras al-Khaimah, was a formidable force, though their land allies, the Saudis, had just withdrawn their forces from Buraimi following the Egyptian destruction of the first Saudi state. The Qawasim fleet was estimated to contain more than sixty large craft and several hundred smaller vessels with some 20,000 skilled sailors and ferocious fighters. Although the British men-of-war carried heavier guns, the Arab vessels were faster, more maneuverable, and of shallower draft, and their crews knew the shoals, reefs, and hidden outlets of the Gulf. However, in November 1819 a mixed British-Indian force of 3,000 men and three British naval ships, backed by the Sultan of Oman's fleet and land forces, attacked Ras al-Khaimah, destroying ships and fortifications there and, subsequently, in Dubai, Ajman, and Sharjah.[24]

THE BRITISH IMPERIUM AND THE TRUCIAL STATES THROUGH WORLD WAR I

The defeat of the Qawasim confederation led to the signing of the General Treaty of Peace in January 1820 that was, through extension and modification, to form the basis of the British position in the Gulf for a century and a half. The ruler of Bahrain as well as the ruling shaikhs of the northern coast of Oman pledged themselves to maintain lasting peace between their tribes and Britain. They also accepted clauses prohibiting slavery and cruel treatment of prisoners; the treaty further stipulated that ships of the maritime tribes would be freely admitted to British ports. There is an understandable tendency among Arabs looking back at these events today to ascribe cynical motives to the lofty principles that the British enshrined in the treaty.[25] The treaty obviously served British self-interest, and the British attempt to impose moral standards that were relatively new in the West might seem hypocritical. However, because the treaty was also sensibly magnanimous and aimed at securing the interests of all parties, it effectively ended piracy in the Gulf.

Article 7 of the treaty condemned piracy among the Arab tribes and implied a British obligation to maintain the peace in the Gulf, thus establishing the germ of the trucial system. (Thus, the European usage of the term "Trucial States" to refer to the lower Gulf shaikdoms developed. The usage was not adopted locally.) The trucial system took explicit form in 1835 when raids by the Bani Yas, rivals of the Qawasim, led to British imposition of a truce during the summer pearling season. The truce was made year-long in 1838 and renewed annually until 1843 when it was extended for ten years. A small British squadron policed the truce, but it was essentially self-enforcing because it conferred significant economic benefits. Interestingly, in the conditions of peace that the treaty secured, lower freight rates for Arab ships led to an Arab monopoly of the Gulf trade by the 1840s, which forced the European carrying trade in that region into decline.[26] In 1853 the trucial system was given formal permanency in the Treaty of Maritime Peace in Perpetuity.

The active British involvement in Gulf affairs largely shaped the region's history for the next century and a half. In great part it did so by freezing the power relationships that existed between tribes or tribal confederations, thereby preserving a number of small states that otherwise would probably have been swallowed by larger neighbors. Eventually the British role in the affairs of the Trucial States would carry their evolution toward western-style statehood a step further by defining territorial boundaries. However, the British long resisted any inclination to become embroiled in conflicts on the mainland of Arabia. Thus, their intervention had the effect of benefiting the Bani Yas, a tribe in the western part of the Trucial States whose power was land-based, against the preeminently maritime Qawasim. The rivalry of these factions was the dominant theme of Trucial States policies in the fifty years following 1820.

The Bani Yas

The Bani Yas came originally from Najd, the central part of Arabia and the traditional heartland of Saudi Arabia. Technically they are not a single tribe because the component groups are not descended from an eponymous ancestor. However, the constituent clans had by the time of British entry into Gulf affairs been welded together by a common history of several centuries into a tightly knit federation that acted like a tribe. By the middle of the seventeenth century the Bani Yas, then as now the most numerous tribal grouping in the area of the UAE, controlled most of what is now Abu Dhabi, with the string of Liwa oases as their center.[27] They shared this territory with parts of other tribes, many of whom came seasonally from the north and west in search of grazing lands. One tribe, the Manasir, has been a loyal ally to the Bani Yas from the beginning of the last century and has done so without any loss of its independent tribal identity. Together with other sections of the Bani Yas the Manasir has given allegiance for more than two and a half centuries to the Al Bu Falah, the smallest clan within the Bani Yas, and specifically, to one family of the Al Bu Falah—the Al Nuhayyan.[28]

Most of the tribes, including the Bani Yas, have been characterized by both settled and nomadic elements; the latter, of course, have progressively disappeared in recent decades. In contrast with tribes in some parts of the Middle East, these are not large. By the most generous estimate the Bani Yas, despite their locally dominant numbers, were only about 15,000 as of the late nineteenth century. (Their numbers are considerably smaller today.) The other tribes generally boasted fewer members, some numbering only in the hundreds. They seem almost tiny when measured against the great tribes and confederations of central and northern Arabia—the Shammar, Anayzah, and Utayba—let alone the huge numbers of the Bakhtiari or Qashqa'i in Iran. However, the alliance of the Bani Yas and the Manasir in the nineteenth century provided strength of numbers against the rival Qawasim and their allies.[29]

The Consolidation of Bani Yas Power

The Bani Yas had begun to expand and consolidate their domain from an early date. Discovery of water on Abu Dhabi island in 1761 made permanent settlement along the coast of what is now the Emirate of Abu Dhabi possible for the first time and added a new dimension to the economic and strategic situation of the Bani Yas, who thenceforth participated in the pearling trade in maritime warfare as well. The town, which became the seat of the Al Bu Falah ruling shaikh in the 1790s, grew a population of several thousand in the course of the last century. Although an attempt early in the seventeenth century to gain a foothold in al-Ain (or Buraimi) Oasis failed, by the early nineteenth century the Bani Yas were making considerable efforts to bring that area under their control. This brought them up against expansionist Saudi power.

Buraimi, as the strategic key to invading Oman, was a principal object of successive Wahhabi occupations during the first three quarters of the nineteenth century. The first, as we have seen, ended with the temporary eclipse of the first Saudi state in 1819. Subsequently, the rulers of Abu Dhabi effectively gained the support of various tribal groups in the Buraimi area, especially the Manasir and Dhawahir tribes. From 1833 to 1839 another period of Wahhabi control ensued, ending when the second Egyptian expedition was mounted against the Saudis. In 1848 the Bani Yas–led confederacy drove the Wahhabi forces from Buraimi after another three year occupation. Following a brief reoccupation and expulsion in 1850, there was a final Saudi attempt to invade Oman in 1853 and a renewed occupation of the oasis that lasted until 1869. Subsequently, the leader of the Bani Yas, Shaikh Zayed bin Khalifa, known as Shaikh Zayed the Great (ruled 1855–1909), consolidated the preeminent Bani Yas position in the oasis.

In the 1950s when oil exploration had established the need for defined national borders and made border location a matter of great practical interest, control of the Buraimi area became an issue of international importance. On the basis of Wahhabi collection of *zakat*, an alms tax traditionally levied on an Islamic ruler's subjects, Saudi Arabia was to claim that the oasis fell within its territory. (The Buraimi dispute and its consequences are examined later in this chapter.) What is certain is that by the last two decades of the nineteenth century Shaikh Zayed had established the dominance of the Bani Yas in Buraimi and firm control over the rest of Abu Dhabi, i.e, the area that the shaikdom now occupies. In so doing he had made Abu Dhabi the dominant power among the Trucial States, thereby supplanting the Qasimi federation.

Shaikh Zayed's forceful leadership was a crucial factor in promoting Bani Yas predominance into the twentieth century. However, it was the death of the great Qasimi patriarch, Shaikh Sultan bin Saqr, in 1866 that opened the way to Zayed's triumph. Even before Sultan's death, at the age of eighty-five, the Qasimi federation, which embraced several important coastal settlements and numerous tribes, was partially split up among the old ruler's sons at Sultan's behest. The senior branch of the family continued to rule in Sharjah while other family members established themselves at Ras al-Khaimah and at Dibba and Kalba on the Batinah (Gulf of Oman) coast.[30] Despite their fall from regional dominance, the Qawasim shaikhs continued to maintain their position in the northern area of the Trucial States where the more rugged terrain helped them to defend against the intrusion of Bani Yas power. In 1850 the Qawasim reached a compromise with the Sultan of Oman, acknowledging his authority over the Musandam promontory that juts out into the Strait of Hormuz, leaving Qawasim rule undisputed in the area north of a line between Sharjah in the west and Kalba in the east.[31] Thus, although bested in their contest with the Bani Yas, the Qawasim retained a powerful presence in the Trucial States.

Moreover, the Bani Yas had already suffered a defection that would lead to a new rivalry that supplanted the old one with the

Qawasim. In 1833 a subsection of the Bani Yas called the Al Bu Falasah seceded from Abu Dhabi and settled in Dubai, until then a dependency of Abu Dhabi. One of the two leaders of the secession, Maktum bin Buti, established the dynasty that continues to rule Dubai. Although hard pressed to preserve its independence from threatening Bani Yas and Qawasim neighbors, the new shaikhdom possessed an excellent natural harbor (in contrast to Abu Dhabi) and by the late nineteenth century was the leading commercial center on the lower Gulf coast. Dubai's rivalry with its former Al Bu Falah overlords has continued in various ways to the present.

The Growth of British Influence

As we have seen, the external influence of the British on events in the Trucial States grew by stages after 1820. As the significant internal developments in the Gulf were occurring in the late nineteenth century, a series of political, strategic, and legal moves that further extended British sway over the Trucial States were taken. As with so many other chapters in the expansion of the British imperial system, what happened in these shaikhdoms was more the product of accident than design.

Problems in the operation of the economically vital pearling industry, which flourished under the conditions imposed by the treaties of 1820 and 1853, led to the establishment of further British control over local affairs. Disputes about absconding pearl merchant debtors led the Trucial States to adopt the suggestion of the British political resident in Bushire—the senior British official in the Gulf—to sign an agreement calling for mutual surrender of such malefactors when they took refuge in neighboring shaikhdoms (see Chapter 4 for a further discussion of the pearling industry). In accepting the terms of the 1879 agreement, Abu Dhabi, Sharjah, Ras al-Khaimah, Ajman, and Umm al-Qaiwain acknowledged a further measure of British tutelage and took another step toward acquiring a collective political identity that separated them from the other Gulf states.[32]

Between 1887 and 1892 the threat of European rivals in the Gulf led to "exclusive agreements," which capped the long series of treaties that formally established British influence and control in the Trucial States. In 1871 the Ottoman Empire sent an expedition to occupy al-Hasa in eastern Arabia, which was the main factor in promoting the British position in the Gulf. A bit later, real or imagined French, German, and Russian intrusions persuaded the British that more formal definition should be given to their relationships with those Gulf states with which they had established special relationships.

Thus, they drew up agreements with the Trucial States that culminated in the treaty of March 1892, which bound the rulers not to yield any territorial sovereignty without British consent. Britain, moreover, assumed responsibility for the foreign relations of the shaikhdoms and thus, by implication, for their protection.[33] This treaty, definitively marking Britain's shift from commercial to strategic concerns in the Gulf, became the principal legal/diplomatic pillar of British authority in the Trucial States. While their European rivals challenged Britain's position there and throughout the Gulf—which these rivals saw being turned into a "British lake"—diplomacy and a bit of judiciously applied cooercion confirmed an unchallenged British dominance in the Gulf.

As legal and political actions were tightening British control over the Trucial States, technology in the form of telegraphic communications was reinforcing the economic and political ties between Europe and the Gulf during the last four decades of the nineteenth century. Moreover, the opening of the Suez Canal in 1869 and continuing advances in steam navigation, by facilitating the movement of merchant marine and naval ships, helped to make the local powers in the Gulf still more readily susceptible to external influence and control. These developments might have been expected to present a greater challenge to the British position in the Gulf. That they did not was due mainly to the limited degree of outside commercial interest in the region at that time. Thus, Britain, through its colonial Government of India, maintained without serious challenge its exclusive position in the Gulf. As the twentieth century progressed Britain continued to preserve the status quo of the Trucial States (and other Gulf shaikhdoms), further strengthening the coastal rulers with which British officialdom was in contact and intervening more frequently in the affairs of the coastal rulers. By the end of World War I the defeat of the Ottoman Empire and Britain's dominant position in the Arabian Peninsula and the Gulf had made Britain more than ever the arbiter of Trucial States affairs.

DEVELOPMENTS BETWEEN THE WORLD WARS

Despite the rise of independent, nationalist regional powers in the Gulf area—Saudi Arabia, Iraq, and Iran—British control over the Trucial States (and the other states in special treaty relationships with Great Britain—Kuwait, Bahrain, Qatar, and Oman) remained essentially undisturbed in the period between the world wars. This was so mainly because the three large, independent Gulf states were preoccupied with the process of nation-building and of coping with serious internal threats. Nevertheless, Iran under Reza Shah pressed claims to the islands of Abu Musa and the Tunbs, which belonged to Sharjah and Ras al-Khaimah respectively. (These are the islands that Iran, under Reza's son Mohammed Reza Pahlavi, seized in December 1971. On brief occasions in the late nineteenth and early twentieth centuries Iran occupied the islands before being forced by the British to relinquish them.) Moreover, Saudi Arabia, taking advantage of the weakness of Abu Dhabi's rule in the interior following the death of Shaikh Zayed the Great in 1909, sought again to impose its authority in the Buraimi (al-Ain) area. Indeed, some tribes there paid *zakat* to the redoubtable Abdullah ibn Jiluwi, governor of al-Hasa province in eastern Saudi Arabia, in return for his protection, though Saudi Arabia did not reoccupy the oasis.[34] Abu Dhabi maintained its position in the Buraimi area and under the rule of Shaikh Shakhbut bin Sultan (1928–1966) reasserted its full control over its interior. However, fear in Abu Dhabi of the growing power of Saudi Arabia (the name adopted by the Saudi state in 1932) and its territorial ambitions continued.

If the rulers in Abu Dhabi and the other shaikhdoms, in the years after World War I, lost some of their capacity to control the tribes away from the coast, at the same time their capacity to act as independent rulers was being further curtailed by the British. In part this reflected a shift in British interest away from the Iranian side of the Gulf, where Reza Shah's nationalist assertion of power undercut the British position. It also reflected the growth of British commercial and imperial communications interests, such as air route facilities. A residency agent in Sharjah already exercised great authority with the rulers. He was an Arab national and, like his superior—a British political resident in Bushire, Iran (later moved to Bahrain)—he was a servant of the British Government of India. Britain's power in the lower Gulf was codified in a series of agreements in 1922 that obligated the Trucial States rulers to grant oil concessions only to companies approved by the British government. Even more restrictive was a 1937 ultimatum by the political resident forcing all the rulers to deal only with Petroleum Concessions Ltd., a wholly owned subsidiary of the London-based Iraq Petroleum Company (IPC), itself partly owned by the Anglo-Iranian Oil Company (AIOC).[35] The ultimatum was less a reflection of British interest in further discovery of more Middle Eastern oil (England then had an adequate supply) than it was an expression of British desire to keep other parties out of the economic and political affairs of the Trucial States. The agreements might thus be seen as symbolizing the considerable degree of isolation that British protection imposed on the Trucial States.

Nevertheless, in the 1920s and 1930s there were developments that had the opposite effect of increasing these states' exposure to and interaction with the outside world—at least in a limited way. For the small literate segment of the population, newspapers from Cairo and elsewhere were imported, bringing news of events in other parts of the Arab world and introducing Arab nationalist ideas at a time of general ferment. This added to a modest intellectual and cultural development stimulated by increased ties with Egypt after the opening of the Suez Canal and, in the opposite direction, by contacts with Bombay resulting largely from the pearl trade. As part of a local cultural revival, poetry enjoyed a certain efflorescence in Dubai and Sharjah.[36]

However, the Trucial States only were linked to the outside world in a significant way through the establishment in the early 1930s of a British air route along the Arab side of the Gulf. Between 1932 and 1936, after overcoming a degree of resistance from the rulers involved, the British established facilities in several of the Trucial States for both military and civilian aircraft. The airport constructed in Sharjah in 1932 established the first physical British presence on the Trucial Coast—a symbol of the British move away from noninvolvement in the affairs of the local states beyond the edge of the Gulf waters.[37] In fact, the British desire to secure an emergency landing ground in Kalba, on the Gulf of Oman, led the political resident to overcome his moral doubts and recognize the local leader's independence from Sharjah, despite Britain's recognition and protection of that state, thereby creating a new emirate. (In 1952 Kalba was reabsorbed by Sharjah.)[38] Especially in Sharjah, where the site of the aerodrome used by Imperial Airways was located, regular contact with Europeans began to have a cultural impact, particularly on those Emirians with some education.

The opening of the Gulf air route had another important consequence for the Trucial States: It altered the position of their rulers. No longer in a purely passive situation of accepting British mediation and protection, these rulers had entered into a new kind of relationship of permitting air route facilities to be built in their territories, by undertaking to safeguard them, and by receiving money for doing so. The last of these new circumstances was especially important as it represented another source of income for the rulers, one independent of their subjects (for the first time). This was particularly significant as it occurred when the decline of the pearling trade and the worldwide depression of the 1930s had brought economic hardship to these shaikhdoms. The local rulers' positions were strengthened, starting a process that would continue into the oil bonanza of the 1960s and 1970s.

Just as the air route in the Gulf was established, oil was being discovered in Bahrain, and a transformation of its economy began soon after. Shaikh Shakhbut of Abu Dhabi especially was eager that exploration be carried out in his domain. He and the rulers of Dubai and Kalba signed oil concession agreements with a subsidiary of IPC before World War II; other rulers did so in the 1940s and 1950s.[39] Though no oil in commercial quantities was discovered until the 1960s, the payment for exploration rights was another source of new wealth and strength for the rulers. Perhaps even more important, the signing of the concession agreements indicated, for the first time, the need to establish precise political borders where previously only a vague sense of territoriality existed for either Gulf-oriented coastal dwellers or interior bedouin populations. In a modest way, at least, these developments presaged the establishment of modern nation-states. They also generated disputes, one of which became a major international issue—the Buraimi Oasis dispute.

The Reform Movement

Another development of the interwar period that helped to set the stage for social and political change in the era of oil wealth was the reform movement and its promotion of innovation in Dubai in the 1930s. Following its secession from Abu Dhabi in 1833, Dubai, without significant hinterland, survived and prospered by pursuing positive relations with the British and by allowing its sophisticated and well-connected merchant community free rein. Decades before oil was discovered Dubai was the largest and wealthiest town of the lower Gulf coast, a multiethnic city-state whose prosperity derived principally from the pearling and re-export trade. It was the good fortune of this mercantile city-state to be governed by a wise, progressive ruler, Shaikh Maktum bin Hashar, at the turn of the century when new commercial opportunities were arising. He and his successors were paternalistic merchant princes, ruling virtually without any administrative structure. This worked well until discontent caused by a decline of prosperity in the Great Depression and the example of reform elsewhere in the Gulf led to the Dubai reform movement of 1938–1939.

Most of the reformers were from the ruler's own extended family of several hundred. Influenced by political developments elsewhere in the Arab world and drawing on the model of the successful reform movement in Kuwait, in October 1938 they forced the shaikh to accept a consultative council (*majlis*). With fifteen members chosen by the notables of Dubai, and serving under the presidency of the ruler, the *majlis* attempted both practical reforms as well as enlightened political and social innovations. The customs service was regulated, the harbor improved and expanded, a municipal council created, and the first real schools in the Trucial States established. Shaikh Said bin Maktum saw the reform movement essentially as a form of opposition to him personally, and the *majlis* did serve as a vehicle for pursuit of narrow self-interest as well as for disinterested reform. After five months of the *majlis'* existence the shaikh was able to force its dissolution.[40] However, the example of the brief experiment and the dynamic mercantile environment that produced it were later to generate lasting reforms and progress and served as the foundation of Dubai's current prosperity and as a challenging example to the other Trucial States of successful urban development.

THE LAST PHASE OF BRITISH PROTECTION: FROM WORLD WAR II TO INDEPENDENCE

In the two and a half decades after World War II, although elsewhere in the Middle East they were in retreat, the British became most closely involved in the affairs of the Trucial States. This seems more anomalous still in light of the fact that the British position in India, a century and a half before, was responsible for the establishment of preponderant British influence in the Gulf, and thus it might have been supposed that, with Indian independence in 1947, British concern with the Gulf and protection of the Trucial States would end. For a number of reasons British interests continued and solidified.

One scholar has argued persuasively that the British stayed on largely through force of habit.[41] Such a feat of inertia was possible in a part of the Middle East that lacked a nationalist movement and where British protectors and local rulers had developed a mutually convenient and comfortable relationship. However, there were other more dynamic reasons for the continued British presence. Even if the imperial links with India had been severed, Britain still maintained important outposts east of Suez with which communications through the Gulf area had to be safeguarded. Further, with the onset of the cold war, Britain, as a member of the Western alliance, was part of the bulwark against Soviet expansionist designs (as inherited from the tsars) in the region. But the most compelling determinant of the continued British presence was probably oil, both as a strategic interest to be protected and as the cause of intensified border disputes among the Trucial States that compelled British involvement.

When exploration for oil resumed in the postwar years on a larger scale than before, the question of how far a particular ruler's territorial authority extended became a matter of intense material interest. One example was an Abu Dhabi–Dubai dispute in which the issue of concessionary boundaries was further complicated by tribal feuds in the same area. Both states signed agreements with Petroleum Development (Trucial Coast)—or PD(TC), the name assumed in 1936 by Petroleum Concessions Ltd.—before World War II and staked out overlapping territorial claims. The dispute, held in abeyance during the war years, broke into open conflict in 1945 when renewed oil exploration stirred up tribal feuds into which the rulers of the two states were drawn. The conflict came to a head in early 1948 when a raiding party from Dubai killed fifty-two Manasir allies of Abu Dhabi. This prompted the participants to come to terms on a border from the coast to the interior laid down by the British (a further portion of the border remained in dispute beyond independence). As one scholar observed, this marked the first time that the British government had deliberately involved itself in Trucial States affairs on land. A much larger and more serious issue, the Buraimi dispute, led to a full embrace of this basic shift in British policy.

The Buraimi Dispute

The Buraimi dispute was significant also because it involved a challenge to sovereignty over the bulk of Abu Dhabi's territory. Saudi Arabia based its claims on earlier occupations going back, as we have seen, to 1800. The dispute was precipitated by the initiation of oil exploration in the area where each side challenged the other's sovereignty. Britain's role as protector of Abu Dhabi (and Oman and Qatar, parts of whose territory were also in dispute) put it at odds with Saudi Arabia. In addition, because the United States was partial to the Saudi claim, the Buraimi issue was a significant irritant in Anglo-U.S. relations in the Middle East.

As with many other border disputes in the Arabian Peninsula, the immediate cause was exploration for oil. The consequent need was to establish precise boundaries where shifting tribal allegiances had defined a ruler's writ before. In the 1930s the California Arabian Standard Oil Company (CASOC), renamed the Arabian American Oil Co. (Aramco) in 1944, and the Anglo-Persian Oil Co., parent of PD (TC), raised the issue in trying to define their respective concession areas (i.e., areas in which the companies had rights to explore for oil and gas). The matter remained dormant until 1949 when Aramco survey parties penetrating east of Qatar prompted Abu Dhabi's ruler,

Shaikh Shakhbut, to complain to Saudi Arabia. Although in the late 1930s Britain's desire to secure Saudi friendship in the face of Mussolini's Ethiopian aggression and the revolt in Palestine disposed it to be conciliatory, a decade later London met expansive Saudi claims with more extensive Abu Dhabi claims.

More important than possible oil reserves to King Abdul Aziz ibn Saud of Saudi Arabia was his belief that the whole inland area of eastern Arabia, as distinct from the settled coastal area, was properly Saudi territory. This rested on the nineteenth-century Saudi expansion into this part of the peninsula via conquest and conversion of local tribes to the tenets of conservative Wahhabi Islam. The Saudis maintained that these tribes remained loyal to them despite the considerable lapse of time since the end of actual Saudi control eighty years before. Thus, they were little disposed toward compromise, while Britain was now prepared to defend wide Abu Dhabi claims to protect its clients' interests and those of the London-based oil consortium exploring there.

A 1951 British-Saudi agreement to establish a frontier commission that would determine tribal loyalties in the disputed area led to a conference for that purpose in early 1952 that adjourned without reaching agreement. That August the dispute reached a crisis point when the Saudis dispatched Turki ibn Utaishan to Buraimi as their local political representative accompanied by forty armed retainers. Following British protests, the Saudis reinforced their party, and the Sultan of Muscat sent the recently created Trucial Oman Levies to take Buraimi by force. Fighting was averted when agreement was reached on a U.S.-proposed "stand-still agreement," which embodied an undertaking to renew negotiations on the frontier. (The United States acted as a concerned friend to both sides.) Finally, on July 30, 1954, an arbitration agreement was signed to set up an independent tribunal to determine the common Saudi-Abu Dhabi frontier. The international tribunal, chosen by both sides, met in September 1955 to hear and adjudicate the claims.

Considerable historical evidence was brought forth in both the Saudi and British memorials to support the claims of both sides. The impressive scholarly resources of the research division of Aramco were devoted to developing the case for Saudi Arabia, which rested principally on establishing tribal loyalties as demonstrated through payment of the Islamic tax, *zakat*, to representatives of Saudi rulers. No determination was ever reached, and the paucity of records and the ambiguities of control or influence by either side make any current objective determination of sovereignty over Buraimi and the other disputed territory during the period in question extremely difficult.

It is clear that the Saudis controlled Buraimi for much of the first seven decades of the nineteenth century and exerted influence over that area in the 1920s and perhaps later. Yet the Bani Yas and the Omanis had contested Saudi control in the last century, and Saudi occupation between 1800 and 1869 was divided into five separate periods and never reestablished until the expedition of Turki ibn Utaishan in 1952.

After the final expulsion of Saudi forces from Buraimi in 1869, the Bani Yas established a strong position there (see the section on "The Consolidation of Bani Yas Power). Yet, here also the degree and continuity of control over the tribes in the area were questionable. Although Lorimer, a prime source, at one point stated that Buraimi after 1869 became "almost an annexe" of Abu Dhabi, his other observations are at variance with this one.[42] Moreover, in the 1940s, even with the capable and respected Zayed as his brother Shakbut's representative in Buraimi, the Abu Dhabi government could not prevent fractious tribes from harassing oil exploration teams. Further, there was evidence of continuing Saudi influence among several tribes in the area.[43]

In any event, the evidence did not determine the issue. Shortly after the tribunal convened, the British member, Sir Reader Bullard, resigned on the grounds that Shaikh Yusuf Yasin, the Saudi member of the tribunal and deputy foreign minister of Saudi Arabia, was in effective control of the conduct of the proceedings for his government and, therefore, was completely partial. Bullard's resignation led to the collapse of the proceedings after which, on the advice of the British government, the rulers of Abu Dhabi and Oman reoccupied Buraimi, using the Trucial Oman Levies to compel the Saudi force there into surrender and withdrawal. The British indicated that they would henceforth consider the de facto frontier to be the Riyadh Line, a border that the British had proposed in 1935 and revised in 1937.

Subsequent attempts to settle the issue through negotiation failed, although Britain still had its protective relationship with Abu Dhabi and Oman. The controversy deeply strained Saudi-British relations. U.S. partiality toward Saudi Arabia, where Aramco was a vital U.S. interest, contributed to a souring of Anglo-U.S. relations in the period leading up to Suez. Much later, in 1970, as events were moving quickly toward British withdrawal from the Gulf, the Saudis reiterated their territorial claim to a great part of Abu Dhabi, including most of its onshore oil fields. As will be seen below, the Buraimi question defied settlement for several years after UAE independence, constituting a major issue of contention between the new state and Saudi Arabia.

British Institutional Presence

If Buraimi dramatically drew the British into full involvement in the basic affairs of the Trucial States, beyond the traditional sphere of the Gulf and its littoral, other less dramatic forms of involvement had important and lasting consequences as well. In the years after World War II Britain upgraded its political presence in the Trucial States and created several institutions that in the relatively brief time before withdrawal of British protection helped prepare the way for independence.

Shortly before the war a British political officer was for the first time appointed to Sharjah, which had been served by an Arab residency agent. (The political officer was directly under the authority of the political resident, who was the senior British representative in the Gulf. Thus, the new appointment reflected a more direct British interest and involvement in Trucial States affairs.) From 1948 on the political officer abandoned the earlier concession to comfort and health and remained in Sharjah year round, not just in the cool months. In that same year the British Foreign Office assumed responsibility for the conduct of Britain's relations with the Gulf states. (Never having been colonies or protectorates, these states could not come under the mandate of the Colonial Office.) In 1953 the greater development of oil company and official British involvement in the Trucial States caused the British representative in Sharjah to be raised to a political agent. A year later he was moved to Dubai and in 1961 was joined by another political agent in Abu Dhabi (where from 1957 to 1961 the rank had been that of political officer). This last development reflected British anticipation of expanded Trucial States development in the wake of the first oil discoveries. However, the general upgrading of British representatives came as responsibilities multiplied. After 1950 the political agent served as judge of His/Her Britannic Majesty's Court for the Trucial States. He also chaired the meetings of the Trucial States Council.

The first major institutional reflection of expanded British involvement in Trucial States affairs was the creation of the Trucial Oman Levies (TOL) in 1951. Originally a very small British-officered force drawn largely from the Trucial States, especially Abu Dhabi, its mission was to keep peace and order throughout the shaikhdoms and serve as an escort for the British representative. The force was formed in particular to provide security in the hinterland for prospecting oil men as well as to protect aircraft and their passengers in Sharjah and prevent abduction of women and children for slaves. The TOL soon established sufficient safety in the Trucial States to enable the free movement of foreigners and, as noted above, was called into action during the Buraimi crisis.

During the mid-1950s the TOL was expanded to about 1,000 men and its name changed to Trucial Oman Scouts (TOS). The bulk of the soldiers came from Oman, especially the western province of Dhofar, and in 1957–1959 fought in Oman itself to assist the forces of the sultan against his rival, the imam, in the interior of the country. Apart from that campaign the TOS confined its activities to the seven Trucial States, frequently undertaking various civilian tasks, including road building, in addition to its police duties. When the UAE was formed, this efficient force of 1,700 men provided the basis for the new nation's army, helping to start the process of integrating the member states' separate defense forces. Those defense forces—in Abu Dhabi, Sharjah, Ras al-Khaimah, and Dubai—were also largely British-officered, with both seconded and contract officers. (Seconded officers are on government assignment; contract officers are on a private arrangement.) Thus, the British, through official policy and otherwise, assumed nearly total responsibility for the internal and external security of the Trucial States.

It was a year after creation of the Trucial Oman Levies, in 1952, that the Trucial States Council was established, bringing together the rulers of the seven states. Initially, the British political agent presided, but by the mid-1960s the chairmanship rotated among the rulers. Although this body was only consultative, wielding no real power, it played a significant role in providing for the first time a forum in which the rulers met as equals to discuss matters of common concern. Thus, for two decades before the UAE came into being, an important level of communication and deliberation among the ruling shaikhs was established, providing a modest but highly important element of integrative nation-building. A sense of unity was engendered that was to prove highly useful.

In addition, under the aegis of the council for 1965, a Development Office carried out important infrastructural projects supported by a development fund to which Britain, Kuwait, Bahrain, and Qatar initially contributed. The lion's share of financial backing soon came from Abu Dhabi, which had by the mid-1960s become a significant oil exporter. In the years leading up to independence the Trucial States Development Office, if on a modest scale, accomplished vital work in health services, education, communication, and agriculture. With very modest funds (by later standards), vital services were inaugurated and a foundation established for long-term development planning and its funding.[44]

Although some might fault the British for not doing more sooner for the people of the Trucial States, they did an effective job of creating institutions or prototypes of institutions that have served the independent UAE well. In addition, the British helped create habits of cooperative thought and action that proved crucial later in helping to sustain the fledgling union. Indeed, new developments in communications and education promoted by the British not only helped pave the way to integrated independence but provided a sense of membership in the wider Arab nation as well, though these were not foreseen or intended results.

Modernization and a New Era

At the same time, while British initiatives provided the basic thrust and context for political, social, and cultural development, much of the impetus for these developments came from indigenous sources. The considerable progress made in Dubai before World War II has already been noted. The advantages of being a compact city-state with a sophisticated, energetic business community, when combined with Dubai's favored position as residence of the British political agent, briefly gave that shaikhdom the leading role before independence in pointing the Trucial States toward a new era.

Shaikh Rashid's initiative in promoting modernization of the port during the 1950s provided a fillip to Dubai's trade-based prosperity. This made possible advances in a number of areas—Dubai provided the only modern medical care in the lower Gulf in the 1950s, built on the educational innovations of the 1938–1939 reform movement, established a police force, and set up a modern municipality to provide structure and order to its rapid growth. As impressive as any other accomplishment was the manner in which Dubai coped with the massive influx of immigrants from Arab and South Asian countries beginning in the mid-1950s, drawn by Dubai's burgeoning development.

Other shaikhdoms also began to show their commitment to modernization. With British assistance Sharjah began in 1953 to provide truly modern schooling for the first time in the Trucial States. Moreover, in Sharjah in 1969 a local, nationalist press was established for the first time in the lower Gulf when the Sharjah daily *Al-Khaleej* (The Gulf) was launched. Ras al-Khaimah's Shaikh Saqr bin Muhammad also took a leading role in promoting education. Both Said Ghobash, former UAE minister for planning and current director of the Arab Monetary Fund, and his uncle, the late Saif Ghobash, who was UAE minister of state for foreign affairs, were among the products of this schooling.

By the mid-1960s Abu Dhabi's oil-derived wealth enabled it to catch up with Dubai's earlier economic lead. Beginning in 1966, when the conservative Shakhbut, fearful and suspicious of modernization, yielded the position of ruler to his more adaptable younger brother Zayed, Abu Dhabi pursued broad, fast-paced development. This was reflected in the rapid expansion of its administration, budget, and defense force—the Abu Dhabi Defense Force—which soon grew to outnumber the Trucial Oman Scouts. Shaikh Zayed gave some of Abu Dhabi's first university graduates positions in the government, among them Ahmad Khalifa al-Suwaidi, who was appointed chairman of the Emiri Court, which played an important role in Trucial States affairs and in the development of Abu Dhabi.

The Beginning of British Withdrawal

However, despite the onset of rapid development during the 1960s in Abu Dhabi, Dubai, and Sharjah as well as the creation and evolution of important economic and political institutions for the Trucial States overall, there was no compelling pressure to abandon the special protected relationship with Britain and pursue complete independence. The rulers were comfortable with a situation that had served their interests well for a century and a half. Although there were some initial stirrings of nationalist sentiments that ran counter to an indefinite continuation of this last vestige of the British Raj, London's role in Trucial States affairs could have continued essentially unchallenged for some time.

The impetus for relinquishing Britain's long-standing responsibilities in the lower Gulf came instead from the British government in reaction to the increasingly burdensome cost of its strategic defense engagements east of Suez. In the words of one scholar, "A blow in the pocket thrust Britain from the Gulf."[45] With Labor in power under Harold Wilson, a White Paper on defense policy was issued in February 1967 reflecting the party's longstanding determination to trim defense expenditures by closing most military bases east of Suez. Yet initially, although withdrawal of troops from Aden and the South Arabian protectorates was already scheduled for 1968, the commitment to maintain the special British position in the Gulf remained alive. Indeed, preparations were made for a slight augmentation of forces in the Gulf to meet the remaining obligations after the withdrawal from Aden. This was reaffirmed in July 1967 when a Supplementary

Defense White Paper was issued. Six months later, however, the Labor government implemented stringent proposals for domestic and foreign expenditure cuts that in Chancellor of the Exchequer James Callaghan's initial plan would have brought immediate withdrawal from the Gulf. When announced in Parliament on January 16, 1968, the proposals called for departure from the Gulf by the end of 1971. What changed the situation was the worrisome deterioration in the country's balance of payments, which had brought on a November 1967 devaluation of the British pound.

Many observers felt that the few million pounds spent annually to maintain the British forces in the Gulf were cost-effective insurance for the £2 billion in annual Western oil company revenues. However, political weariness with the residual burdens of empire and the adoption of a nuclear-age military establishment that brought with it severe cuts in personnel reinforced the ostensible financial logic of abandoning the Gulf. Thus, Britain's manner of withdrawal was rather like its mode of entry into the Gulf—a spin-off of broader policy considerations and not a result of a conscious, deliberate design for the Gulf.

The liquidation of the last remnants of the Raj in the Middle East may not have been one of Britain's finest moments. Indeed, it might smack of abandonment considering that the rulers of the Gulf states were eager to retain British protection—Shaikh Zayed even offered to contribute funds from his own oil revenues to maintain the British presence.[46] However, the painful abandonment of other imperial responsibilities in the Middle East suggested that there was wisdom in a voluntary departure from a still relatively somnambulent backwater that would not always remain so. The June 1967 War and the anti-British sentiment that it generated gave further point to such a consideration.

What is most open to criticism is the degree to which the withdrawal decision was made a political football: Actual British intentions were not made clear until only a few months before withdrawal. The surprise electoral victory of the Conservative party in June 1970 delayed a definitive announcement of intended British actions in the Gulf while the new government scrutinized its original opposition to withdrawal. Although the Conservative party had attacked Labor's decision to withdraw as "scuttle," on March 1, 1971, the government announced that British forces would be withdrawn in December.

Although the Conservative government can be faulted for the confusion resulting from its delay in determining a Gulf policy, it would not have been feasible to reverse Labor's decision. To have kept British forces in the Gulf after promising their withdrawal might well have served to generate the instability the forces were meant to prevent. Moreover, the larger states of the Gulf were opposed to reversal of Britain's commitment to withdraw; only Shaikh Rashid among rulers of the nine protected shaikhdoms would publicly call for such a course of action—and then only obliquely.[47]

Even if it seemed advisable in 1971 for Britain to go through with its Gulf withdrawal, observers expected that there would be greater disruption immediately afterwards than at any time during the century and a half of the Pax Britannica in the region. There were indeed compelling reasons for such fears—the protected Federation of South Arabia had quickly succumbed to an armed takeover by Marxists; the Popular Front for the Liberation of the Occupied Arab Gulf (PFLOAG) posed an imminent threat to Oman and, linked with radical Ba'ath Iraq, appeared to be only a slightly longer range danger to the shaikhdoms in the Gulf; and the daunting number of outstanding territorial and dynastic disputes among the Gulf states seemed to presage more trouble than a fledgling state could manage. Yet, however inauspicious the situation, the seven Trucial States, Qatar, and Bahrain began discussion in 1968 to consider the formation of a federation in which they could combine their resources despite an uncertain future.

THE TRANSITION TO INDEPENDENCE: A FEDERATION OF NINE OR SEVEN?

Writing in 1966 a distinguished journalistic observer of the Middle East declared emphatically that "there is no realistic possibility of the present Gulf rulers coming together of their own accord in any political grouping worth mentioning." He thought the prospects of Britain's pushing them into doing so equally discouraging.[48] Although this dismal prediction seemed likely to come true in the confused and uncertain aftermath of Britain's 1968 announcement of withdrawal from the Gulf, the difficult course toward attempted union began right after the announcement and created what would prove to be a viable federation by the time British protection had been withdrawn.

The British favored a federation of nine—the seven Trucial States plus Qatar and Bahrain—which would have the presumed benefits of a larger population and the inclusion in its administrative structure of Bahrain's trained civil servants. With luck these attributes would help preserve a new state against potentially threatening neighbors. Shaikh Zayed of Abu Dhabi and Shaikh Rashid of Dubai also wanted to include the two other states because of the close ties that they enjoyed with Bahrain and Qatar respectively. Thus, the February 18, 1968, agreement between Abu Dhabi and Dubai to form a federation— covering foreign affairs and defense as well as internal matters— contained an explicit invitation to all the other seven rulers to join them. Only a week later all nine rulers met and, moving initially with surprising speed, adopted a draft constitution presented by Qatar as the basis of a union to be called the Federation of Arab Emirates. It envisioned a rather loose grouping of the nine states in which the rulers could act only with a unanimous vote.[49]

During the next year and a half several meetings of the nine rulers, who together constituted the Supreme Council of the proposed federation, met without making much real progress toward agreeing on and establishing its institutions. On October 21, 1969, a meeting in Abu Dhabi of the rulers was supposed to elect Shaikh Zayed as the federation's first president and Shaikh Rashid as its first vice president, establish Abu Dhabi as its temporary capital, determine on the creation of a permanent capital on the border between Abu Dhabi and Dubai (the name of the site selected was not propitious— Wadi al-Mawt, or Valley of Death), and select Qatar's Deputy Ruler, Shaikh Khalifa bin Hamad, as prime minister. However, the meeting broke up without issuing a communiqué, and the nine rulers never again met together as the Supreme Council. The ostensible reason for the breakup of the meeting was the delivery of a message from the British political resident in the Gulf, Sir Stewart Crawford, indicating that the British government would be very disappointed if the rulers did not overcome their difficulties in moving toward federation. The rulers of Qatar and Ras al-Khaimah walked out of the meeting, claiming British interference. The real reason for their walkout, however, was fear of larger neighbors' reactions to implementation of the proposed federation of nine. Iran, which had put forward a claim to Bahrain as part of its territory, may have warned some rulers against proceeding with their plans. Its position was certainly clear the day after the meeting adjourned when it announced that a federation including Bahrain was "unacceptable" until Bahrain's status was settled in accordance with accepted international principles.[50]

The Iranian claims to Bahrain were laid to rest by the finding of a U.N. investigation, made public in May 1970, that Bahrainis wanted an independent sovereign state. This removed a major motive for Bahrain's desire to join the federation—protection from Iranian irredentism. At the same time, several of the rulers feared joining a federation with Abu Dhabi while Saudi Arabia again pressed its claim to some four-fifths of that emirate's territory. Following the British election of June 1970 and the attendant expectation that the Conservatives might reverse Labor's policy of withdrawal, there was still less disposition to press toward federation. Bahrain and Qatar proceeded to build up their own administrative/legal structures, anticipating the prospect of going it alone as independent states. Although the British government continued to delay an announcement of its Gulf policy, Sir William Luce's October 1970 mission to the Gulf rulers left them persuaded that withdrawal would occur. Although Saudi Arabia and Kuwait mounted diplomatic efforts until April 1971 to promote a federation of nine, it was clear by then that the prospects for such a federation were doomed.[51] On August 15, 1971, Bahrain declared its independence, and two weeks later Qatar did the same.

In the meantime, on July 1, Shaikh Zayed, sensing the collapse of efforts to promote a wider federation, established Abu Dhabi's first cabinet and took the first steps to set up a fifty-member National Consultative Assembly. The ruler's son, Shaikh Khalifa bin Zayed, was designated prime minister. A bright young commoner, Dr. Mana Said al-Otaiba, was appointed minister of petroleum, the post he still retains. Abu Dhabi's action prompted the other six Trucial States to meet on July 10 to discuss forming a union of all seven. On July 18 it was announced that the State of the United Arab Emirates had been formed. Anticipating the important role it would play as an aid donor in the Arab world, Abu Dhabi had two days earlier established its Fund for Arab Economic Development. The UAE came into being without Ras al-Khaimah. For a variety of reasons that state opted at the outset to remain outside the union.

The Problems of Independence

With a bit more than four months until independence the new state had thus been formed with three of the anticipated members declining to join. Moreover, there was a nearly total lack of trained manpower to run the country and a variety of other daunting problems. Although the UAE's territories were almost entirely contiguous, there were no modern roads across the mountains to the Gulf of Oman coast nor even between the UAE's two main political and economic urban centers of Abu Dhabi and Dubai, which were divided by 100 miles of desert. In addition, a host of disputes between the various ruling families, largely about the complex patchwork of ill-defined borders, threatened to undo the fragile new entity before it was properly launched. At the same time, external threats were even more menacing. The collapse of a British-sponsored federation in South

Arabia in 1968 was an unhappy precedent that brought to power in Aden a radical, Marxist government that was bent on overturning all conservative governments in the area. Iran, having accepted a face-saving retreat from its claim to Bahrain, was now determined to brook no interference in pressing its claims to three islands belonging to Sharjah and Ras al-Khaimah. Finally, Saudi Arabia continued to press its claim to most of Abu Dhabi's interior.

Launching a wealthy but militarily defenseless and politically undeveloped ministate into this sea of troubles could be seen as an exercise in long odds. However, one way or another, they were successfully defied. Although territorial and other disputes between the emirates' rulers still persist, Shaikh Zayed and Shaikh Rashid established a fruitful precedent in February 1968 by resolving some of their mutual claims.

Although it could not be foreseen at the time, the radical leftist forces in the region that appeared poised to threaten seriously the conservative regimes in the Gulf had reached their high watermark. By 1975 the Dhofari rebellion in western Oman, supported from Marxist South Yemen through PFLOAG, had been contained by the Sultan of Oman with important British, Iranian, and Jordanian military assistance. PFLOAG's loss of vitality would be reflected in its sub-sequent, much more circumspect name—Popular Front for the Liberation of Oman (PFLO). Also in 1975, Iraq, whose radical Ba'thist government had sought to destablilize the conservative Gulf regimes, signed the Algiers Accord with the shah of Iran, thereby settling outstanding differences with Iran and launching Iraq on a more moderate and pragmatic course. Despite the ostensible radical leftist threat to the region, however, as December 2, 1971, the date of British withdrawal, approached, the Iranian claims were the most menacing cloud on the horizon.

Iranian Territorial Claims

The Iranian claims to three small islands strategically located just inside the Strait of Hormuz were weak. Abu Musa had been ruled as part of Sharjah for at least a century and the Tunbs as part of Ras al-Khaimah during an equivalent period of time. On various occasions Iran had asserted claims, all of them rejected by the British who, especially under the terms of the 1892 treaty, had a legal obligation to defend the Trucial States from aggression. Indeed, an Iranian occupation of the islands in 1904 had quickly ended with a rapid British assertion of sovereignty on behalf of Sharjah and Ras al- Khaimah.[52] Iranian claims had remained dormant after World War

II until the announcement of Britain's intention to withdraw from the Gulf. The Shah was by then committed to establishing Iran as a protector of the Gulf and its Indian Ocean approaches. He genuinely feared the radical threat to the region—which his military was then helping to check in Oman—and he did not trust what he foresaw as a weak, unstable Arab state to secure strategic islands against the threat of hostile forces. An opportunity to reassert Iranian authority was undoubtedly compelling and, politically, the Shah was not in a mood or position to yield after relinquishing his claims to Bahrain. Possible oil finds may have been a factor in the Shah's position, but strategic and political issues seem clearly to have been more important.

The British, in the face of Iran's statement that it would oppose the federation if its claims were not satisfied and occupy the islands by force if necessary, tried to promote a compromise solution. On November 29, 1971, the issue of Abu Musa was, indeed, settled in this fashion.[53] In regard to the Tunbs it was a different story. Shaikh Saqr bin Muhammad of Ras al-Khaimah refused to make a deal with the Shah and on November 30, the day before the British treaty of protection was to expire and the UAE become independent, the Iranians seized the Tunbs by force, killing four Ras al-Khaimah police and losing three of their own men. (On the same day they made a peaceful landing on Abu Musa.) No meaningful Arab reaction was possible against Iran; there was insufficient Arab military power to accomplish such a challenge, and Britain was still the protecting power at the time of the attack. Britain suffered the brunt of general Arab anger—Iraq broke diplomatic relations, and Libya, on December 7, nationalized British Petroleum's assets and producing interests in Concession 65 and withdrew all its deposits from British banks.

The manner in which the issue of sovereignty over the islands was settled proved acutely embarrassing for the British and generated spontaneous demonstrations of hostility toward the Shah and Iran in the UAE (Iran still holds the Tunbs). However, the effects of this were not lasting or significant. Britain retained close and friendly ties with the UAE after relinquishing its responsibilities as protector, and British relations with pre-Khomeini Iran soon became reasonably friendly. Although the issue of sovereignty over the islands still remains a potential source of area tensions today, it did not torpedo the launching of the independent UAE the day after the Iranian seizure.

Resolution of the Saudi Arabia–Abu Dhabi Border Dispute

Although less dramatic than the Iranian threats and actions concerning the islands, the Saudi claim to large tracts of Abu Dhabi territory, including most of its onshore oil deposits, was potentially more serious. It will be recalled that since the breakdown of negotiations in 1955 the Abu Dhabi–Saudi border was an administrative line unilaterally declared by the British. The Saudis never accepted it, and in May 1970 King Faisal bin Abdul Aziz al-Saud proposed to Shaikh Zayed a settlement involving somewhat less extensive claims than the Saudis had earlier pressed. The new proposal, however, would still have deprived Abu Dhabi of several oil fields. It also required a plebiscite to determine sovereignty over Buraimi Oasis, which had long been dominated by Abu Dhabi's rulers and was Zayed's birthplace over which he had presided as governor until 1966. This last was a particularly sensitive point with him. King Faisal's deep historical memory and Saudi sensitivities were involved as well because of nineteenth century Wahhabi proselytizing and military successes in the Buraimi area and beyond. Indeed, a throughtful examination of the evidence suggests that these considerations had much more to do with the insistence of Saudi claims than did the prospect of adding marginally to the already vast Saudi oil reserves. Finally, the memory of Saudi forces driven out of Buraimi by the Trucial Oman Levies, led by British officers on behalf of Abu Dhabi, rankled sorely.[54]

The issue was not resolved for three more years. By then the important shared interests of the two states in the security and stability of their traditional systems of government against common threats led them to an accord on July 29, 1974. Saudi Arabia renounced its Buraimi claim but was given a corridor to the Gulf between Qatar and the UAE at Khor al-Udaid, territory formerly claimed by Abu Dhabi, and the two states agreed to share the disputed Zarara oil field.[55] Although this agreement has yet to be given public formal announcement, it did at last banish the principal obstacle to friendly relations between Abu Dhabi and Saudi Arabia.

A Federation of Seven

Finally, the new nation had to start life with one of the former Trucial States, Ras al-Khaimah, outside the union. That state, proud of its past, felt resentment at not being accorded equal political weight with the larger states in negotiations about the terms of unification. In addition, it was still pursuing settlement of the Tunbs issue and retained hope that rumors of an offshore oil strike would shortly be confirmed. However, in February 1972, with hope of oil wealth dashed (until 1983 when oil in commercial quantities was discovered) and federal financial support of its development projects assured, Ras al-

Khaimah agreed to become the seventh member of the UAE. On December 2, 1971, when the UAE became independent, there was no assurance that Ras al-Khaimah would join or that other internal and external difficulties and uncertainties might not engender centrifugal forces that would cause the fragile new nation to break apart.

These circumstances might have seemed to justify the pessimistic prediction made a few months before the launching of the UAE that "whatever happens the Gulf has already entered a period of flux in which neither existing boundaries nor traditional regimes can be expected to prevail."[56] The UAE and its neighbors have thus far given the lie to that minatory forecast, partly through simple good fortune and partly because of the quality of their leadership. In the case of the UAE, Shaikh Zayed's capacity to project traditional leadership values while comprehending and accepting the challenge of absorbing rapid changes have proved critical. His sharing of Abu Dhabi's wealth with the poorer shaikhdoms reflected both the instincts of traditional Bedouin generosity and the capacity for calculating the integrative development needs of an infant federation. Although the state institutions inherited by the UAE were few and incompletely developed, they, too, helped to preserve it in its early trials. Indeed, the UAE's governmental authority continues to derive from a provisional constitution adapted from the one that had been proposed for the projected nine-member federation in 1968.

NOTES

1. Geoffrey Bibby, *Looking for Dilmun* (Harmondsworth, England: Penguin, 1980, first published in 1970).

2. For a report on some recent investigations of early links between lower Gulf and Indus Valley civilizations, see "The Indus Valley Connection," *The Middle East*, no. 107, (September 1983).

3. Bibby, *Looking for Dilmun*, p. 229.

4. Ibid., p. 393. See also K. G. Fenelon, *The United Arab Emirates: An Economic and Social Survey*, 2d ed. (London and New York: Longman, 1976), p. 122.

5. Bibby, *Looking for Dilmun*, p. 298.

6. Ibid., pp. 267, 345-346, 384, 390, 392. The location of the fabled city of Gerrha is another absorbing question. Gerrha remained an important trading city at the junction of several major trade routes until the middle of the second century B.C. under the Seleucids. See Kamal Salibi, *A History of Arabia* (Delmar, N.Y.: Caravan Books, 1980), p. 37.

7. Michael Tomkinson, *The United Arab Emirates: An Insight and a Guide* (London: Michael Tomkinson Publishing, 1975), pp. 165–166; and *The Gulf News* (Dubai), March 18, 1981.

8. Tomkinson, *An Insight and a Guide*, p. 9.

9. *Arab Oil*, no. 11 (Kuwait, November 1982):18.

10. Frauke Heard-Bey, *From Trucial States to United Arab Emirates* (London and New York: Longman, 1982), pp. 21–22.

11. Roger M. Savory, "The History of the Persian Gulf: The Ancient Period," Alvin J. Cottrell et al., eds., *The Persian Gulf States: A General Survey* (Baltimore and London: Johns Hopkins University Press, 1980), pp. 12–13; Donald Hawley, *The Trucial States* (London: George Allen and Unwin Ltd., 1970), p. 25; and Salibi, *History of Arabia*, p. 73.

12. S. B. Miles, *The Countries and Tribes of the Persian Gulf*, vol. 1 (London: Harrison and Sons, 1919), p. 38.

13. Roger M. Savory, "The History of the Gulf: AD 600–1800," Cottrell, *Persian Gulf States*, pp. 15–17. The quotation is from Tim Severin, *The Sindbad Voyage* (New York: C. P. Putnam's Sons, 1983), pp. 15–16.

14. George F. Hourani, *Arab Seafaring in the Indian Ocean in Ancient and Early Medieval Times* (Princeton, N.J.: Princeton University Press, 1956), p. 83.

15. See Alan Villiers, *Sons of Sinbad* (New York: Charles Scribner's Sons, 1969, originally published in 1940), pp. 395–396.

16. Tomkinson, *An Insight and a Guide*, p. 184; and Hawley, *Trucial States*, p. 71.

17. Savory, "History of the Gulf," p. 38.

18. Malcolm Yapp, "The History of the Persian Gulf," Cottrell, *Persian Gulf States*, p. 45; and Salem al-Jabir al-Sabah, *Les Emirats du Golfe: Histoire d'un Peuple* [Emirates of the Gulf: History of a People] (Paris: Fayard, 1980), p. 64.

19. See, respectively, Sir Charles Belgrave, *The Pirate Coast* (London: G. Bell and Sons, Ltd., 1966), p. 27; and Ahmed Ubaidly, "The Military Expedition against Ras al-Khaimah, 1819–1820," *Gulf and Arabian Peninsula Studies* (in Arabic) 8, no. 31 (July 1982):163–184.

20. Savory, "History of the Gulf," p. 48.

21. Hawley, *Trucial States*, p. 117.

22. Miles, *Countries and Tribes*, p. 315.

23. Ibid., p. 323.

24. See especially Belgrave, *Pirate Coast*, pp. 33, 56, 135–143, whose account is based on the diary of a British ship's captain who participated in the expedition.

25. See, for example, Ubaidly, "Military Expedition," p. 179.

26. J. B. Kelly, *Britain and the Persian Gulf* (London: Oxford University Press, 1968), p. 369.

27. Heard-Bey, *From Trucial States to Emirates*, pp. 42–43.

28. Ibid., pp. 45–46; and J. B. Kelly, *Eastern Arabian Frontiers* (New York and London: Frederick A. Praeger, 1964), pp. 38–39.

29. The previously cited works of S. B. Miles and J. B. Kelly as well as J. G. Lorimer, *Gazetteer of the Persian Gulf, Oman, and Central Arabia*, 2 vols. (Calcutta: Superintendent Government Printing, 1915) provide detailed

information on the size, importance, and shifting alliances of the several dozen tribes in the UAE area in the nineteenth and twentieth centuries. Heard-Bey offers a detailed discussion of tribal dynamics and their impact on UAE society in chapters 1 and 2 of her abovementioned book.

30. Sir Rupert Hay, *The Persian Gulf States* (Washington, D.C.: The Middle East Institute, 1959), p. 123.

31. Heard-Bey, *From Trucial States to Emirates*, p. 82.

32. Ibid., pp. 291–292.

33. Ibid., p. 293; and Malcolm Yapp, "British Policy in the Persian Gulf," Cottrell, *Persian Gulf States*, pp. 80–82. Dubai adhered to the 1892 treaty as did the five shaikhdoms that signed the 1879 agreement. See also Husain M. Albaharna, *The Arabian Gulf States: Their Legal and Political Status and Their International Problems*, 2nd. revised ed. (Beirut: Librairie du Liban, 1975), pp. 29–30.

34. Rosemarie Said Zahlan, *The Origins of the United Arab Emirates: A Political and Social Study of the Trucial States* (New York: St. Martin's Press, 1978), pp. 80, 82, 84.

35. Ibid., pp. 20, 27, 66, 118–120; and Heard-Bey, *From Trucial States to Emirates*, p. 295.

36. Muhammad Morsy Abdullah, *The United Arab Emirates: A Modern History* (London and New York: Croom Helm and Barnes and Noble, 1978), pp. 106–108.

37. Heard-Bey, *From Trucial States to Emirates*, pp. 298–299.

38. Rosemarie Said Zahlan, "The Gulf States: A Historical Perspective," pp. 17–18. This paper was presented at a seminar on February 10, 1982, for the Gulf Project of the Center for Strategic and International Studies, Georgetown University.

39. Zahlan, *Origins*, pp. 108–111; and Heard-Bey, *From Trucial States to Emirates*, pp. 296–297.

40. Heard-Bey, *From Trucial States to Emirates*, pp. 254–257; and Zahlan, "The Gulf States," pp. 25–26.

41. Yapp, "British Policy in the Persian Gulf," p. 94. Indeed, Yapp sees this as the primary reason for Britain's continued presence and maintains (p. 98) that there was no really conscious strategic design sustaining the British position in the Gulf.

42. Lorimer, *Gazetteer*, pp. 770–771; and see Albaharna, *The Arabian Gulf States*, p. 213, where the discrepancies between several of Lorimer's statements are cited.

43. Heardy-Bey, *From Trucial States to Emirates*, p. 301; and Albaharna, *The Arab Gulf States*, pp. 217–218. In *Arabian Sands*, (New York: Penguin, 1980), pp. 271–272, Thesiger observes that Zayed's "authority was strong in the mountains and in all the towns, but was weak among the large and powerful Bedu tribes of the Duru and Wahiba who live on the steps bordering on the sands. Ibn Saud had undisputed control over the Murra beyond the Sabkhat al-Matti and his officials sometimes collected taxes from the Bedu who lived in Dhafara. But recently they had been driven out of Liwa by the

Bani Yas, who acknowledged Shakhbut as their overlord. . . . Now the only Saudis here, i.e. Buraimi, were a few merchants engaged chiefly in the slave trade which still flourished in the two villages not controlled by Zayed."

44. A detailed exposition on the Development Office and its projects is provided in Heard-Bey, *From Trucial States to Emirates*, pp. 319–335.

45. Yapp, "British Policy in the Persian Gulf," p. 95.

46. J. B. Kelly, *Arabia, the Gulf & The West: A Critical View of the Arabs and Their Oil Policy* (New York: Basic Books, 1980), p. 49.

47. David Holden, "The Persian Gulf: After the British Raj," *Foreign Affairs* 49, no. 4 (July 1971):729.

48. David Holden, *Farewell to Arabia* (New York: Walker and Company, 1966), p. 159.

49. The text of the agreement is in Albaharna, *The Arabian Gulf States*, pp. 380–383.

50. *Middle East Economic Survey* 13, no. 1 (October 31, 1969) and 13, no. 2 (November 7, 1969); and Heard-Bey, *From Trucial States to Emirates*, pp. 345-353.

51. *The Arab World*, no. 4415 (April 21, 1971), and no. 4419 (April 27, 1971).

52. See Abdullah, *A Modern History*, pp. 244–245. A review of the legal issues may be found in Albaharna, *The Arabian Gulf States*, pp. 339–348.

53. Sharjah's ruler, Shaikh Khalid bin Muhammad, had, on August 23, sent to other Arab states a memorandum citing Sharjah's established and long-standing rights to possession of Abu Musa and sought their support against Iran. Reportedly only four states responded, all urging restraint. The texts of the memorandum and the Iran-Sharjah agreement are in *Middle East Economic Survey* 15, no. 6 (December 3, 1971).

54. John Duke Anthony, *Arab States of the Lower Gulf: People, Politics, Petroleum* (Washington, D.C.: The Middle East Institute, 1975), p. 148. In *The United Arab Emirates: Unity in Fragmentation*, (Boulder, Colo.: Westview Press, 1979), p. 204, footnote 20, Ali Mohammed Khalifa quotes King Faisal as saying to Shaikh Zayed: "The whole thing to us is a matter of dignity and honor. The British evicted us by force and we won't forget that." Thus, no agreement had been reached at the date of UAE independence, and Saudi Arabia ominously withheld diplomatic recognition.

55. Anthony, in *Arab States of the Lower Gulf*, pp. 148–149, indicates that the oil field would be divided while Khalifa, on p. 149 of *Unity in Fragmentation*, states that the agreement called for the field to be within Saudi territory but that it is unclear whether it stipulated joint oil exploration or ownership of the oil by one country or the other. Neither the terms of the agreement nor a map reflecting its territorial alterations has yet been published.

56. Holden, "The Persian Gulf," p. 734.

3

Society and Culture

The UAE, like its oil-rich neighbors, presents a bewildering blend of traditional and modern elements in its cultural and social life. At a superficial glance, ideas and tastes of the contemporary West, symbolized by the vast array of imported goods and services that are avidly consumed, would appear to be obliterating what remains of the conservative, indigenous culture. Many Emirians fear that this is in fact already happening, and most observers would probably agree that over time the UAE's greatest problem will be to preserve enough of the basic values of its society to keep it from being simply swept away by an avalanche of change. Nevertheless, what is perhaps most striking are the strength and resilience of the basic elements of traditional society—Islam, the tribe, and the family. These continue to shape the society and culture of the UAE.

Islam

Some thirteen hundred fifty years (fourteen centuries according to the Islamic lunar calendar) after the arrival of Islam in what is now the UAE, Islam remains the most important formative, cultural influence. By contrast with religion as generally practiced in the modern secular West, Islam is a complete prescription regulating the conduct of the individual and the society. The essential beliefs and practices of Islam are relatively simple. They can be summed up in the five "pillars": (1) *shehada*, the bearing of witness to the uniqueness of God and his sending Muhammad as his messenger; (2) the *haj*, the annual pilgrimage to mecca; (3) *salat*—prayer performed five times daily; (4) *saum*—fasting during the month of Ramadan; and (5) *Zakat*—the payment of a religious tax. No attempt will be made here to describe the rich and complex culture that is based upon the Quran (God's message delivered to Muhammad) and the *Sunna* (actions and

59

sayings of the Prophet) and that reflects varieties of symbiotic relationships with elements of pre-Islamic cultures. Islam provides the
framework of existence for all in the community as well as the essence
of moral and spiritual authority. Application of the Sharia, the body
of Islamic law, is intended not merely to enjoin correct behavior
preparatory to the afterlife but to define and regulate state and society
on earth. Even though the theoretical unity of state and religion has,
from earliest times in Islamic history, yielded in practice to a division
between political leaders and religious leaders, the ideal has continued
to shape perceptions and behavior. The UAE is a relatively conservative
Muslim country in which Islam remains a powerful factor in shaping
the political, social, and cultural life. In this sense it offers a contrast
to those Arab states such as Egypt, Iraq, and Syria—much longer
exposed to secularizing influences—even though Islam obviously
remains an important factor there also.

Most Emirians are Sunni (orthodox) Muslims, though there are
some Shia Muslims of Iranian origin (not including several thousand
Shia non-nationals resident in the UAE).[1] From neighboring Oman,
Ibadism, a schismatic survival from the very early Islamic period and
separate from both Sunni and Shia Islam, has exercised some influence.
The dominant Sunnis are divided among those following the Maliki
school of theology and law, officially recognized in Abu Dhabi and
Dubai; adherents of the Hanbali school, recognized in the other
emirates; and adherents of the Shafi'i school, found only in Fujairah.
It is important, however, not to exaggerate the significance of the
theological and legal differences between the schools. More noteworthy
is the degree of homogeneity among Sunnis in the emirates; even
though Hanbalis are somewhat stricter and more conservative, they
are generally less austere than their cousins of the same school in
Saudi Arabia. (The Wahhabis found in the al-Ain area, reflecting
Saudi occupation in the last century, follow the Hanbali teachings.)
Divisions that have occurred between Malikis and Hanbalis have
reflected the differences between the tribal confederations—Hinawi
and Ghafiri; these tend to be aligned with the two schools respectively.

The role of Islam in state and society is reflected in the several
kinds of formal status accorded to it. Islam is recognized as the formal
religion of the UAE in the provisional constitution, which also
acknowledges the Sharia as a principal source of legislation. Because
the federal court system outlined in the constitution is not yet
established, the traditional religious judges, or qadis, have retained
principal responsibility for the administration of justice. At the federal
level the formal connections between religion and justice are sym-

bolized in the grouping of matters relating to justice, religious affairs, and religious endowments (or *awqaf*) in a single ministry.

Although Sunni Islam as practiced in the UAE is conservative and, since the Iranian revolution, its norms of prescribed behavior have been more forcefully imposed, it does not exhibit an extremist face. It is true, nevertheless, that the more self-conscious and intense assertion of Islamic values, recently witnessed throughout the Muslim world community, has been noticeable in the UAE as well. "Even so," one scholar noted, "the so-called 'fundamentalist' activities [in the UAE] have been less in evidence than elsewhere."[2] There are proponents of a reinvigorated assertion of Islamic values in high official positions, and Shaikh Zayed and the other emirate rulers are broadly perceived as embodying and defending Islamic values. But generally, in the UAE, Islam serves more to support the political system than to threaten governmental stability or survival. This helps to insulate the country from the shock waves of the Khomeini revolution.

At the same time, the number of Muslim militants in the UAE could grow. In April 1981 a destructive bomb, which killed two people, was set off in the Hyatt Regency Hotel, apparently by Muslim extremists, because that hotel had served liquor to local Muslims in traditional dress, thereby violating a local unwritten rule.[3] This and other less violent occurrences serve as a reminder of the militants' presence and the intensity of their feelings. The federal and individual emirate governments have responded by decreeing measures meant to appease the extremists, e.g., more thoroughgoing sexual segregation in the schools, the imposition of religious law on all Muslims, and harsh traditional punishments, such as whipping (the punishments are especially for crimes of immoral behavior). Generally, however, despite the essentially conservative and pious attitudes of the general population, this sort of extremism is shunned, and compromises are reached in the actual application of sanctions. Most Emirians (as is true of most Muslims) lack a dour or fanatical streak. However, the voices of militant Islam are increasingly heard, particularly at the UAE National University in al-Ain where the militants have found a platform, though they have little real power.

Although the continuing observance of Islamic norms suggests the strength of traditional values, the scope and speed of modernization reveal Islam's general flexibility toward various kinds of change. Thus, Islam should not be regarded as antithetical to the development process. The conservative Hanbali school, for instance, permits particularly wide scope for innovation because its "strict constructionist" approach defines with narrow precision the sources of the Sharia, thereby granting greater latitude to exercise of independent judicial judgment.

The issue that remains open is the degree to which modernization will alter Islam. It is hard to believe that Islam can survive the impact of massive continuing change without itself eventually changing. The resurgence of Islamic assertion reminds us that Islam has remained for all believing Muslims (and, in a real sense, even for those who might pose as secularists) the central reality and touchstone of their existence. Yet the undoubted encroachment of secular values will someday almost certainly reduce the effective sphere of Islam in society, perhaps in the way Western post-Enlightenment society became progressively secularized. For the present and the near future, however, Islam remains the dominant single influence in the society and culture of the UAE.

The Tribe

In the territory of the Emirates, as throughout all of Arabia, the basic political units of traditional society were the tribes. The relative strength of each tribe waxed and waned depending on the quality of its leadership and economic and other circumstances. The relationship between nomadic and settled populations was not, as it is often portrayed, one of simple, continuous conflict but rather a complex, symbiotic set of dynamic links. Indeed, tribes frequently shifted from a nomadic to a sedentary mode of existence—engaging in agricultural or maritime pursuits, or both—then reverting to their former nature. Various forms of cooperation and conflict determined the way in which scarce economic resources were distributed among the tribes. The situation was highly fluid, and there were frequent changes in tribal fortunes.

The interposition of British forces and diplomacy in the lower Gulf beginning in the early nineteenth century progressively froze the balance of power between tribes and tribal confederations, though conflicts continued to occur among them and have even since UAE independence. Fixed territorial boundaries have now replaced the traditional *dirah*, the elastic concept of an area in which a tribe exercised sway. Despite the essentially uncontested authority of the ruling families in each emirate and the virtual disappearance of nomadism, the loyalty of the tribes is still considered important and is actively sought by emiral rulers.

Abu Dhabi has the greatest number of tribal groups, including a few that are still nomadic. As noted in Chapter 2, the traditionally sedentary Bani Yas confederation has long dominated Abu Dhabi.

The ruling Al Nuhayyan family, also known as the Al Bu Falah, is a small subsection of the Bani Yas who forged an alliance in the early nineteenth century uniting the Manasir, Awamir, and Al Jawahir with the Bani Yas. This alliance has since dominated Abu Dhabi society and politics.

Many tribesmen sought employment with oil companies in Abu Dhabi when exploration and production began, and considerable numbers have since found jobs in construction and various service industries. The government is now trying to settle the relatively few remaining nomadic and seminomadic tribesmen. Thus, traditional tribal life, which has disappeared in the urbanized settlements, will soon be consigned to the past altogether. (I recently spoke with a UAE government official from the Manasir tribe who lamented the passing of traditional ways in the al-Liwa Oasis where he had grown up. Almost no younger members of the tribe are acquainted, for instance, with the techniques of date cultivation, and the elders of the tribe must be pressed to convey this knowledge because they assume that, with today's alternative economic opportunities, no one is interested.) The numbers of people who still have an emotional and/or social allegiance to a tribe have, in almost all cases, considerably diminished since the turn of the century. Yet the government continues to be concerned with maintaining positive relations with the tribes, suggesting their continuing importance even in a rapidly urbanizing culture. Continuity with forms of past authority helps to promote stability in the UAE, especially in light of the fact that military and security force personnel are drawn largely from the tribes.

In the other emirates as well tribal identity is still important, though the numbers claiming such affiliation continue to decrease. Relations between Abu Dhabi and Dubai (ruled by a seceded branch of the Bani Yas) and the states of Sharjah and Ras al-Khaimah, which have been long dominated by the Qasimi clan, though in the latter they are a small minority, often reflect a tension born of long-standing tribal rivalries. In Fujairah, however, with much of its population in rugged rural areas, the greatest numbers of its inhabitants are still tribally oriented. There the dominant tribe, from which the ruling family is drawn, is the Al Sharqi. In Umm al-Qaiwain and Ajman single tribes, the Al Ali and the Nuaim respectively, are similarly dominant in society and politics and provide the ruling houses.

One other tribal group bears mentioning because it is so strikingly different from the others. This is the Shihuh, living in the rugged and remote Musandam Peninsula. Their isolation and unique characteristics—linguistic, social, and other—have led to wild speculation about their origins. Some have thought they were of Persian or even of Portuguese descent. In fact, they are essentially Arab, though with some Persian admixture. Most are subjects of the Sultan of Oman, inhabiting the small, strategic Omani enclave dominating the southern side of the Strait of Hormuz, but increasing numbers have drifted into adjacent UAE territory, drawn by employment opportunities.[4] Their remoteness may slow absorption of the Shihuh into the modernizing society outside their rocky fastness, but their extreme poverty will probably render that absorption inevitable.

The Family

If tribes still play an important role in establishing identity and determining the structure of authority in the UAE, the extended family remains the strongest and most cohesive social unit. Among the diverse, autonomous entities that interact in the mosaic of traditional Middle Eastern Islamic society, the family was and remains the most stable and unchanging. Its nature is defined by characteristics preserved in many cases from pre-Islamic times and reflected in and codified by the body of Islamic personal law in the Sharia. Thus, for example, the family has continued to form a single economic unit, a fact of great social significance because the family's economic base reinforces the unity and independence of the family as a social unit. Still more important is the family's capacity, both past and present, to preserve its essential immunity from governmental influence and intervention.

Although these observations about the family are true even for secularized Arab societies, they pertain especially in the traditional peninsula societies. In the UAE the extended family, under the leadership of the oldest male, remains intact. Marriages continue to be carefully arranged within a small social grouping—those in which a young man marries his father's brother's daughter continue to be the ideal. In a way that is hard for members of Western society, which glorifies individualism, to understand, the individual is subordinate to the family—the basis of a "shame" as opposed to a "guilt" culture. Although sin in Western Christian society is essentially an issue of private conscience, in Islam, behavior contrary to moral norms is a matter of collective concern, bringing shame to the family of the sinful individual. In effect, what is immoral is also illegal; the law that governs society is religious law, and immoral behavior is punishable by legal sanction. Whatever erosion may have occurred in certain social values, this basic reality remains unaltered. Children returning from prolonged exposure to the intellectual sophistication of Western universities and the social atomization of Western society go back almost unfailingly to their families and remain obedient to the wishes of elders who almost universally lack formal education.

The family is still the one refuge where an individual can feel secure and within whose confines most of the activities of men as well as women, apart from education and work, take place. The life of the family remains extremely private. (I learned in Abu Dhabi of an Emirian businessman whose non-Emirian Arab business partner of twenty-five years had never been admitted to his partner's home.)

In a society where modern governmental institutions are in a transitional, if not embryonic, state, family identities and ties continue to have prime political importance. Members of ruling families, as would be expected, occupy key governmental positions in the UAE or individual emirates. In addition, commoners who are members of families closely aligned with ruling clans have acquired political and economic prominence. In Abu Dhabi two noteworthy examples are Mana Said al-Otaiba, who has been the UAE's only minister of petroleum and mineral affairs, and Ahmad Khalifa al-Suwaidi, the federation's first minister for foreign affairs. In Dubai, with its traditional, external mercantile contacts, there are important merchant families of non-Arab, principally Iranian, origin wielding political influence, while commoners of the Al Bu Falasah subtribe hold important posts behind members of the ruling Maktum family. Some expatriate Arabs have wielded very significant influence in Dubai, most notably Mahdi Tajer, originally from Bahrain, who became UAE Ambassador to London. In the other emirates the structure of authority and influence continues largely to reflect family and tribal relationships. One important reason for the continued vitality of patriarchal rule is that it is in harmony with the structure and ethos of the society as a whole.

THE IMPACT OF RAPID DEVELOPMENT

The scope and pace of change in the UAE are dramatically evident in the growth of the country's wealth and in the material transformation being wrought by that wealth. Thirty years ago the Emirates, with the exception of Dubai and its modest commercial affluence, were among the poorest societies in the world. The UAE's per capita Gross National Product, oil glut notwithstanding, is one of the highest in the world. The income from oil has enabled the government to establish an advanced welfare state in which all citizens (and, with qualifications, other residents) enjoy free health care, education, and other social benefits. The new wealth, accruing directly to the government, has expanded enormously the impact of government on society. The society's commitment to rapid modernization has caused the physical and social environment to be massively altered.

Old fort in Fujairah. To the left of the fort the remains of a house of the
old town appear. The traditional mud brick dwellings have been replaced
by federally funded concrete structures.

The Shift to an Urban Society

What was an overwhelmingly rural—indeed, to a signficant
extent, nomadic—population a generation ago is now preponderantly
urban.[5] The virtual absence of any physical structure more than ten
or fifteen years old in Abu Dhabi reflects the extraordinary pace of
change; only a few old buildings survive in Dubai and Sharjah. Glass,
steel, and concrete towers give the UAE's cities the appearance of
transplanted Houstons rising above the flat sands of the Gulf. Almost
overnight the greater part of the population has been displaced from
traditional rural (and/or maritime) modes of existence to a setting
of artificially sustained vegetation, broad boulevards, luxury hotels,
and replicated Wimpys, Seven-Elevens, and Burger Kings, where only
a scattering of barasti huts might have been found a generation ago.

In like fashion there has been an equally dizzying acceleration
in the everyday movement of people and in their confrontations,
direct or indirect, with a wide range of novel experiences. Constantly
replenished fleets of Toyotas, Hondas, and Mercedes speed along
some of the best-designed roads in the world that effortlessly connect
recently remote locales throughout the seven emirates. Easy access

by air travel to other parts of the Middle East as well as to Europe and the United States has made those distant places familiar to Emirians whose parents never ventured more than a few miles from their place of birth. Universal education, the availability of daily domestic and foreign press reporting, and constant exposure to television (including videotapes) provide a constant barrage of new ideas, images, and tastes.

Moreover, the products of the wholesale change whose impact is now being felt are in many cases quite ephemeral. Even the imposing new skyscrapers that dominate the urban skylines soon deteriorate in the harsh climatic conditions of the Gulf littorals while automobiles frequently succumb to the ravages of salt and sand-laden winds in two or three years. These outward physical manifestations of the impermanence of what is new symbolize the transitory and uncertain nature of the inner or psychic alterations brought on by the new environment.[6] Yet, the actual effect of these changes on the people of the UAE is not easily discerned. It may still be somewhat early in the process of change to judge what its deeper impact will be. People generally are slower than is commonly assumed to alter the essential features of their belief and behavior even when the familiar landmarks by which they have directed their lives are being rapidly displaced. Further, the extreme privacy in which Emirians conduct their lives may help to mask the profounder human changes that are occurring.

In any event, what has perhaps been most surprising in the course of the UAE's greatly accelerated development is the capacity of traditional society to absorb massive change. Social institutions and cultural patterns have preserved their essential vitality. One writer noted the enduring strength of the family in coping with change:

> The family I had met had gone through an extraordinary revolution. They had been suddenly exposed to the full blast of 20th century manners and things. Other people in other places had simply been smashed by the impact. . . . Here, though, it was different. The Bedu family had met the century head on, but they had been able to deal with it in the family.[7]

Perhaps even more important is the role of religion. Islam provides both the essential explanation of the meaning of individual and collective existence and serves as the stable foundation of society. As one scholar noted, "The centrality of the revelation of Islam puts all subsequent 'facts' of social change into a very subordinate position so that when changes do appear, they are seen as divine manifestations of God's will and are thus accommodated into the existing pattern."[8]

It cannot be doubted, however, that changes are occurring that will greatly alter basic elements of UAE society and culture and, perhaps, eventually threaten their very survival in anything like their traditional form. As in the other wealthy oil states of the Arabian Peninsula, there is little evident connection in UAE society between wealth and work. As one analyst remarks, "The message is clear: 'without effort or self-denial one can simply accept a world made by others.'"[9] As a result, there are incipient signs of the kind of social malaise already evident in Kuwait with its long history of very high per capita wealth and advanced welfarism. Some young men with large amounts of money and leisure at their disposal are tempted to spend them on such things as expensive cars and mistresses and to avoid meaningful employment. Although serious attempts are being made to educate young Emirians for new responsibilities, and there are notable examples of those strongly motivated by a sense of duty to country despite the attractions of a life of ease, the problems brought on by massive sudden wealth will be very hard to manage. In a dramatic way, the enormous foreign presence in the UAE, the result of an insatiable need for imported labor skills, reflects, exacerbates, and causes major social problems.

The Foreign Worker Issue

The political and security threat from the huge numbers of migrant workers in the UAE is most feared and most widely discussed. As an example, a fairly typical editorial in a leading UAE newspaper described migrant workers as a "fifth column."[10] Such fears are natural in a country where foreigners outnumber natives by more than four to one. An attempted coup in Bahrain in December 1981—aided and abetted by Iran but mounted by native Bahraini and a few other Gulf Arab Shias—has certainly exacerbated those fears. However, it will be argued here that the possible social and cultural consequences of the human tidal wave now engulfing the emirates represent the greater danger. An erosion of traditional values has almost certainly begun, stemming in very large measure from the sudden massive influx of a variety of foreigners whose physical presence and introduction of alien tastes and ideas constitute a major disruptive social force in the UAE. In the long run, this process, if unchecked, could have major political and security consequences and could pose a threat to the stability of the state.

The presence of foreigners, of course, has grown out of the need for skilled technicians and managers to direct the country's development effort, which must be satisfied almost wholly from outside the UAE. The greater number represent the workers of various skill levels who perform labor that UAE natives are not numerous enough (nor generally disposed) to do (such as construction work, taxi driving, and dock work). Commitment to an extremely rapid pace of development, accelerated by the enormous upsurge in oil revenues in the mid-1970s, led to nearly unchecked growth in the number of foreigners—Europeans and Arabs from beyond the Gulf did work that Emirians were not trained for, and Asian laborers did the kinds of work that natives were unwilling to do. Thus, by the start of the 1980s UAE nationals had come to represent perhaps as little as 15 percent of the total population and in Abu Dhabi and Dubai were estimated to account for not much more than 5 percent of the work force.[11] Fear of compromising economic privileges and of diluting their identity has led natives of the UAE, as in the other wealthy Gulf Arab countries, to reject the option of absorbing immigrants as citizens. Thus, in coping with the problem the UAE resorts to palliatives meant to control the size and ameliorate the negative consequences of the large foreign population while hoping eventually to rely on the UAE's own human resources. That, of course, assumes success in overcoming attitudinal as well as educational constraints.

Migrants from other Arab countries are most feared as constituting a potential political threat. The bulk of skilled and unskilled workers has come from Asian countries, most from Pakistan, India, and Sri Lanka, reflecting traditional ties and geographic proximity between the lower Gulf and the Indian subcontinent.[12] But increasingly, capable and hard-working East Asians including Koreans, Filipinos, Chinese, and Thais are sought because of their work skills and habits and because, in contrast to workers from the subcontinent, they do not bring their families or seek to establish permanent residence. Indians, in particular, have tended to settle down, often with working wives, and they form major communities in Dubai and in Abu Dhabi at al-Ain.

If the UAE government (and its neighboring governments on the Arab side of the Gulf) has reduced the level of political risk by substituting Asian for Arab labor, it has probably increased the general threat to the nation's social and cultural values. The introduction into the country of enormous numbers of outsiders, not sharing or even familiar with the customs, traditions, and norms of moral behavior of UAE society, has caused an increase and exacerbation of potentially serious social problems. One is struck by the number of newspaper reports of criminal activity by Asian immigrants involving violence, drugs, and sex. A typical item from the *Khaleej Times* of August 8,

Filipina hotel employee. Rapid economic development and a shortage of indigenous labor skills have resulted in massive dependence on expatriate workers, mostly from other Arab countries, Iran, India, and Pakistan. In recent years workers have come from as far away as the Philippines and South Korea.

1981, was headed "Jailed for Molesting Child," and contained, in addition, accounts of check fraud, fornication, and the sale of pornographic films. Three months later the same paper carried a report on the largest drug raid in Sharjah's history in which 441 pounds of various drugs were seized. The nationalities of those involved in these two cases—Pakistani, Iranian, Indian, and Sri Lankan—were typical of other cases reported in the press.

Although the actual level of criminal activity, particularly by Western standards, appears modest, its scope and nature are new and unsettling to UAE society and create an exaggerated perception and fear of the potential dangers posed by the foreign population. Citing social crime, especially among the male bachelor laborers now forming a majority of the population in the UAE's larger cities, the newspaper *Al-Khaleej* has urgently called for tackling the immigration issue before it causes an explosion. Extrapolating from the recent expansion of the foreign presence, that publication projected that by the year 2000 citizens would constitute only 2.5 percent of the nation's population, becoming strangers in their own country while the outsiders became their masters.[13]

Some thoughtful Emirians are becoming increasingly concerned that the impact of the foreign presence will submerge basic social values and patterns of behavior to the extent that the present generation will be cut off from its heritage. I spoke with a leading intellectual in Sharjah who lamented that his brother's children, looked after by a Filipina nanny, were being raised to speak English (and fragmentary Tagalog), but were unacquainted with their native Arabic. This man was deeply troubled by the prospect of an eventual cultural deracination of the country's young people.[14] Although others might not grasp and articulate this danger as clearly as he, it is undoubtedly sensed very widely, causing deep unease. Indeed, it may well be that cultural alienation of this sort is in fact the single most threatening aspect of the foreign presence.

Although there are no signs yet of widespread popular resentment, there is concern that press attacks on immigrant labor could provoke such feeling. Yet, government officials themselves, when confronted by the continuing need for imported labor and the demands that some way be found to solve the problems such labor generates and avert its potential longer term consequences, are often prey to the same feelings toward outsiders. During a discussion in the federal parliament concerning foreign workers, one member charged that they were spreading doubts about Islam and were responsible for "kidnappings, violations of the sanctity of people's homes, and cultural invasions on the part of Crusaders, Hindus, and Masons." Although this comment may have been deliberately hyperbolic, it conveyed the frustration of other members of the Parliament and Emirians in general.[15] Thus, the government of the UAE is ambivalent toward an essentially intractable issue. The government does provide basic social services to immigrants, including free education for their children, but it has imposed a variety of restrictions and controls in an attempt to control more effectively the flow of human beings into the country. Under the impact of the oil revenue shortfall in 1983 the government ceased providing free medical care to foreign residents except those employed by the federal government, a measure affecting tens of thousands of foreign workers. Yet whatever measures are taken, the need for human brawn and brains and the eagerness of foreigners—especially from poor Asian countries—to exploit opportunities unavailable in their own countries, will perpetuate the problems and the dangers.

Only in the last few years have the concerns of the small, wealthy labor-importing countries led to serious scholarly research

by individuals or interested international agencies such as the World
Bank into the impact and implications of massive labor migration.
Moreover, such research has thus far focused almost exclusively on
economic aspects of the phenomenon. Yet it is increasingly apparent
that social strains are generated not only in the host societies by the
presence of foreign workers, but in the latter's societies as well.
Although many of the Asian laborers live in physically and psychologically difficult situations in the UAE and in its neighbors states,
their wives left at home fall victim to sexual frustration and attendant
disorders dubbed "Dubai syndrome." The prolonged absences of
heads of families cause a breakdown of social controls in some Asian
settings, and the remittances that are sent back often create resentments
and divisions in the workers' home communities.[16] Given the deeply
disruptive potential of the labor migration problem at both ends, the
need for further serious study of its social and psychological as well
as economic impact is obvious. In the final analysis, the greatest
danger of foreign labor is not the "poisonous" ideas and "immoral"
practices that the presence of such labor introduces but the consequences of ingrained dependence on it. The ultimate answer to this
threat must, therefore, lie in measures taken by each nation to create
greater self-reliance.

In the meantime, as noted in Chapter 1, a somewhat positive
feature of the oil glut and the resulting decline in revenues is that
some 200,000 emigrants left the UAE in the early 1980s. Although
this does not provide a solution to the problem of severe imbalance
between native and foreign populations, this exodus should lessen
the strains it has engendered.

Indexes of Social Change

Although the basic elements of UAE society remain intact, there
are already some signs that the disruptive forces of accelerated,
modernizing change are surfacing. One index is the rapidly increasing
number of traffic accidents, to which the endless string of junked
roadside wrecks bears mute testimony. The director general of Sharjah's
police recently commented that the UAE had the highest traffic accident
rate in the world, and there is a widely shared concern about deaths
and injuries on the UAE's roads.[17] Although statistics for 1978 ranking
twelve selected Arab countries, including all the Gulf Arab states,
show the UAE as having the second fewest traffic fatalities per
thousand vehicles, the current situation is reported to be growing
worse. A variety of punitive measures, escalating in severity to
whipping and jailing, has failed to check the rising accident rate.[18]

Among other symptoms of changes in social behavior and values with serious implications for the future are developments affecting the young and the old. It has been necessary in recent years to establish homes for the elderly and rehabilitation centers for juvenile delinquents. These developments are thus far modest in scope, but they represent, in a society as profoundly family-centered as the UAE, a disturbing sign.

Changing attitudes among the UAE's youth should provide one of the obvious indexes to anticipated alterations in the patterns of social behavior, though it is hard to gain any very clear and precise idea in what directions and with what force those changes are occurring. It does seem certain that many of the young people who are returning from study and extended residence in Western countries bring back a greater taste for democratic forms of social and political relationships. Those who attend universities in other Arab countries are apt to develop stronger pan-Arab sympathies and a more intense commitment to issues and concerns in the wider Arab world. Many, whether studying at the UAE National University at al-Ain, elsewhere in the Arab world, or even in the West are drawn to the teachings of militant Islam. In any case, there are signs, as one would expect, of some degree of impatience among younger people with things as they are. Although most of those belonging to the generation now coming of age continue to obey and respect traditional forms of authority, familial and governmental, it seems certain that deference to the paternalistic ways of the past is slowly becoming less automatic. Whether this might in turn evolve into active challenging of authority is difficult to predict, nor is it now possible to say whether bright, young returning graduates will display greater resentment than their generally less-educated elders toward expatriate managers and advisers. Such developments, reflecting the natural impatience of the first postmodernization generation in the UAE, who are less aware than the older generation of the distance their society has already travelled, may be anticipated. How far these developments may go will depend on the degree to which roots linking the young to the past can be preserved.

ASPECTS OF A SOCIETY AND CULTURE IN TRANSITION

Despite the continuing, essential strength of the foundations of UAE culture and society, the dramatic changes in the country's social environment have initiated a process that will, over time, transform the perceptions and behavior of its citizens. Some sense of where that process may lead can, perhaps, be discovered by examining changes in several dimensions of UAE society and culture.

Education

The growth of the educational system and the number of formally educated residents of the UAE constitutes one of the most striking indexes of social progress. The literacy rate is estimated at 60 percent (based on 1980 and 1981 figures) as compared with 52 percent in Saudi Arabia and 99 percent in the United States (1983 figures). There are 73,505 children (of all nationalities) in 283 primary and secondary schools throughout the UAE, more than 2,600 students are at universities abroad, and the UAE National University at al-Ain, with more than 2,500 students, graduated its first class in February 1982.[19] Education is free for all academically qualified children, both nationals and non-nationals, and is compulsory for the former between the ages of six and twelve. The government's massive school-building program and its expansion of teacher training programs since 1983 underscores a continuing commitment to education. As of 1980 the Education Ministry's budget was nearly $300 million, more than 11 percent of the total federal budget. The accomplishments of the UAE in educating its people are striking when one considers that a little more than thirty years ago there were no formal educational institutions in the then Trucial States.

Traditionally, education beyond the inculcation of household and occupational skills and proper social behavior consisted of instruction in reading the Quran, usually at the feet of a local *qadi* (Islamic judge) or other respected religious scholar. As noted in Chapter 2, the first attempt to promote modern education grew out of an indigenous effort in Dubai during that emirate's brief reform movement in the late 1930s. Because the fruits of that effort were short-lived, it was not until 1953 that modern education was in fact established in the Trucial States with the British-assisted inauguration of a school in Sharjah. Soon thereafter Kuwait became the principal external source of aid in building up the incipient educational system. Beginning with the establishment of an Egyptian educational mission in Sharjah in the late 1950s, Arab sources of assistance were preeminent in promoting Trucial States education. This assistance grew out of a sense of obligation and out of a desire to promote educational independence from Britain.

Well before independence several of the Trucial States had begun seriously to promote education with an emphasis on teaching practical skills and building on the start in technical education made when the British established a trade school in Sharjah. The ruler of Dubai soon after launched a similar school, and by the late 1960s both schools were independent of the British government under the Trucial States Development Office. By 1969 there were nearly 300 students receiving technical training in the six northern emirates alone. Until independence Kuwait remained responsible for most of the schools in those emirates. Within a few months of independence this responsibility was vested in the federal Ministry of Education and Youth, which assumed the charge of some 30,000 schoolchildren. Within a decade school enrollment had grown to more than 100,000.

The development of the United Arab Emirates National University at al-Ain has been equally impressive. Opened for the 1977-1978 academic year with four faculties (literature, sciences, political science/public administration, and education), there were 58 faculty members and 447 students (15 percent of the current student population are foreign students). By 1980-1981, 3 more faculties had been added (law and Sharia, engineering, and agriculture), and both faculty and student body had grown nearly fivefold, with women representing nearly 45 percent of the enrollment. The university continues to expand with a long-term projection of 10,000 students. Incentives to study at the university include generous financial support during enrollment and a considerable monetary award at graduation.[20] The federal government's large budgetary outlays for education suggest the importance of its commitment, and the current 60 percent literacy rate indicates the success of the effort to educate the UAE's population.

It is less easy to judge how well the UAE's young people are being prepared for the assumption of specific responsibilities and occupations. In 1980-1981, 70 percent of the total enrollment at the university was in the faculties of literature, education, and political science/public administration. Presumably, graduates in those disciplines will be absorbed into the public sector, though that absorption is less certain for the 30 percent who pursued literary studies—many of those will most likely become teachers. At the same time, with some 20 percent of the university's students in the sciences—mathematics and statistics, physics, chemistry, life sciences, and geology—and some 5 percent in the new faculties of engineering and agriculture, considerable numbers of students are being trained in areas where it is important to develop indigenous skills.[21] What is, perhaps, less certain is how well and in what numbers students studying at the UAE National University or abroad are developing the kinds of managerial skills that will be needed to promote Emirian self-sufficiency in both the public and private sectors.

Additionally, it is not yet apparent what kinds of behavior-shaping influences education will impart. In at least a formal, academic sense a degree of Western, specifically U.S., orientation and influence is evident throughout the educational system. English is taught from the primary grades on, U.S. curricula are studied for guidance in developing the school system, and most university students in the sciences look to advanced study in the United States. Of the 2,600 UAE students who were studying abroad in 1979-1980 (half of them UAE nationals), the United States had by far the greatest number—643. (The United Kingdom was third, with 169, after Egypt.) All faculties of the UAE National University were modelled on the U.S. system—Georgia Tech University advised the engineering faculty on its curriculum—and some faculty members have degrees from U.S. universities. Some lectures are given in English, and each student is required to take general courses in basic English as well as statistics, Arabic, Arabic society, and Islamic thought.[22] Thus, at the university level, many Emirians are significantly exposed to Western, particularly U.S., modes of research and intellectual discourse.

However, the most compelling political and ideological influences come from other Arab cultures. Foreign Arabs have filled most teaching positions at all levels; only recently have they been displaced significantly by native Emirians. As elsewhere in the Arabian Peninsula, Egyptians have played a particularly important role in supplying faculty and administrators. In the schools and the university, local students come in contact with fellow students from other parts of the Arab world, with Palestinians making up the largest foreign Arab contingent in the university student body. One can assume that the UAE students will be to some degree politically radicalized and become stronger Arab nationalists than their elders. In the past two or three years Islamic militants have been a powerful force on campus, as elsewhere in the Arab world, though various factors have somewhat mitigated their impact on the educational or political establishment in the UAE—among them the imposition of male-female student segregation at all levels and the fact that the UAE University president from the university's founding until 1985, Dr. Ezzedine Ibrahim, is himself a respected, conservative religious scholar. Moreover, the university emphasizes law and Sharia studies, with more than 10 percent of the student body (including thirty-two women) enrolled in that faculty.

The capacity and commitment of the state to provide status and material benefits for the products of its educational system have thus far checked any real dissatisfaction or protest from the first generation of formally educated Emirians. Though the generation gap will doubtless be made wider as new habits of thinking undercut traditional outlooks, there is as yet no sign that the educated young are in revolt against the basically conservative, religiously grounded values of UAE society. (An often repeated story has it that in a discussion with students at the UAE National University Shaikh Zayed was asked pointedly why so much of the country's treasure was being spent to plant trees in the desert to little obvious, practical benefit. His answer—"Now you know what trees look like"—would be satisfying to most older citizens, grateful for the amenities that now ease a formerly harsh existence, but from the educated young who increasingly take these comforts for granted more such questioning is likely.) What education has unarguably done is to create a literate society conversant with new ideas and capable of generating social and political change. One important change that education has already inaugurated is the promotion of new social roles for women; female enrollment in the entire educational system is nearly one-half the total, and the government is committed to providing jobs for all graduates.

The News Media: Impact of New Purveyors of Information and Opinion

In its brief history the UAE has witnessed the rapid development of news media, especially newspapers, with some nine dailies (six in Arabic, three in English) serving a total readership of a few hundred thousand. The media are sufficiently free of government control that a variety of views and opinions are presented to the public.

As the large number of newspapers aimed at a small market would suggest, financial subsidization is necessary for them to publish. Two Arab dailies are financed by the UAE federal government and the government of Dubai respectively—Al-Ittihad (Union) and Al-Bayan (Report). The others are supported by private business interests. Although newspapers are read mainly by a local UAE audience, both Al-Ittihad and Al-Khaleej (The Gulf), which is published in Sharjah, are read widely in Qatar, and the latter is also popular in Bahrain and Kuwait. Al-Ittihad has a circulation of 40–50,000, and Al-Khaleej's, though smaller, is in the same range. The rest are considerably smaller.[23] Three English language dailies—The Emirates News, Khaleej Times, and Gulf News (which also puts out an Urdu language paper)—serve the expatriate community. They carry translations of news and editorials from the Arabic press and wire service items, are generally rather colorless, and have no role in shaping UAE opinion.

Much of the Arabic press tends to be quite lively, reflecting a diversity of viewpoints. At the same time, because many of the editorialists are expatriate Arabs, with Palestinians, Syrians, and Egyptians figuring prominently, the press generally tends to reflect a strong Arab nationalist line, including frequent harsh editorial attacks on U.S. policy toward the Middle East. Thus, expressions of opinion in the press are apt to be somewhat to the left of official government policy and of indigenous public opinion.

Al-Khaleej is the most important of the UAE's newspapers and is noteworthy for maintaining a consistent and outspoken line. It takes a firm Arab nationalist position, is strongly supportive of the Palestinians, and tends to be fairly bold in discussing domestic political issues. In addition, *Al-Khaleej*, reflecting Sharjah's cultural and artistic preeminence in the UAE, tries to give prominence to the work of local writers and painters and to cultural activities throughout the Arab world. These factors combine to make it a lively paper that is seriously read and suggest why it competes well against the local press in both Bahrain and Kuwait.

Al-Azmina al-Arabiyya (Arab Times), suspended for some three years (and probably closed permanently), was a news weekly in Sharjah that, like *Al-Khaleej*, adhered to a strong nationalist line, featured forthright opinion on the local scene, and emphasized cultural developments. *Al-Azmina* took the lead, during its several years of publication, in addressing the tough social and economic as well as political issues that others shied away from. It was concerned, for example, with probing the human costs of development.

Al-Ittihad, as its subsidization by the federal government would suggest, is generally a good deal more conservative than the Sharjah publications. The difference in flavor between it and *Al-Khaleej* is reflected in their choices of syndication with foreign news services—*Al-Ittihad* uses the *Times* of London while its Sharjah rival subscribes to *Le Monde*. Both UAE papers maintain foreign stringers; *Al-Khaleej* has a research center and *Al-Ittihad* a less-well developed strategic studies center. Though the newspaper is intended to project a government point of view, *Al-Ittihad*'s editorialists, including numerous Arab expatriates, often express their own viewpoints.

Al-Bayan, funded by the emiral government of Dubai under the editorship of Hasher bin Maktum, nephew of the ruler Shaikh Rashid and a successful businessman, is, perhaps, still more conservative, reflecting the pragmatic business atmosphere of Dubai. It aims at projecting a moderate line on Arab and world affairs and stresses economic news and issues at the local, Arab, and international levels. Through an agreement with the *Financial Times* of London it has access to the reporting of a wide network of correspondents. Some copies of the paper are sold in Bahrain, Saudi Arabia, Kuwait, and

Jordan. *Al-Bayan*'s Middle East Research Center provides research for special supplements on major economic and business issues as well as for the daily issues. In addition to discussing standard issues such as oil and foreign trade, *Al-Bayan* has done in-depth investigative analysis of subjects like abuses in the insurance business and poor management of vocational schools.

Al-Islah, a journal published by a government-subsidized Islamic society represents, by contrast, a conservative religious viewpoint. It has, for example, opposed the teaching of music in the schools, which was supported by *Al-Bayan*, and it attacked the latter, in part because *Al-Bayan* had two Christian editors. Although *Al-Islah* does not have a large circulation, the growth of conservative, indeed fundamentalist, Islamic sentiment in the UAE and the Arab world gives it an importance transcending the size of its readership.

The remaining Arabic papers—*Al-Fajr* (The Dawn), *Al-Wahda* (Unity), and *Al-Watan* (The Homeland)—are less distinctive in their style and contents, though they offer some contrasting viewpoints. They tend to be less well run, in part because their editors are businessmen who do not maintain close control of the papers.

Further variety in the print media is available through the imported press, which is well represented on UAE newsstands. Among Arab papers, *Al-Safir* (The Mediator) and *Al-Nahar* (Today), both from Lebanon, are popular. The major Arabic publications from Paris and London are also fairly widely read. Much of the U.S. and British press is available and read mainly by expatriates. Even when the post–Camp David boycott of Egypt was in full force, Egyptian papers were easily obtainable, catering in large part to the local Egyptian community for social rather than political reasons (see Chapters 5 and 6 for discussions of the Arab-Israeli conflict). Moreover, syndicated columnists such as Mohamed Hassanein Heikal are carried in the UAE press.

Government censorship in the UAE is mild, its press being one of the freest in the Arab world. However, as in Saudi Arabia, self-censorship is practiced in accordance with principles and limits indicated by the government, but there is much testing of the limits of governmental warnings and, occasionally, suspensions when publications overstep the bounds. The aim of government, according to its own dicta, has been to guard against threats to basic cultural values, not to place restraints on how the people, their society, and culture are to be shaped. Although this position leaves open the manner of judging such threats and does not touch on the question of political censorship, it nevertheless provides a general principle that seems to work pretty well in guiding action. It does so because

in practice a pragmatic spirit prevails: The government allows reasonable latitude to the press. The effective indicator of tolerated limits
is WAM (Wikalat Anba al-Imarat), the UAE's news agency (the acronym
is derived from the initials of the Arabic title in Roman transliteration).
WAM's principal function is to collect and distribute local news as
well as choose items from other Arab news agencies for redistribution
in the UAE; its own exclusions provide a guide for self-censorship
by the press.

But if Shaikh Zayed himself encourages free expression of opinion
and exhibits a broad tolerance toward the press, there are frequent
warnings, often from him—usually through a phone call to the editor
of the offending paper—that an editorialist has gone too far on some
sensitive issue. The fate of *Al-Azmina al-Arabiyya*, the only news
publication to be subjected to lengthy suspension, is instructive. *Al-
Azmina* had a history of being well out in front on political and
social issues, and it continually tested the limits of government
tolerance. It pressed the government to assume stronger Arab nationalist positions and to oppose more firmly an expanded U.S.
presence in the Gulf; it also urged the establishment of diplomatic
relations with the Soviet Union. Domestically, it called for a stronger
union and more democracy. In the spring of 1981 *Al-Azmina* played
a key role in helping strikers, including many who worked in agencies
of federal ministries, gain their demands. All this the government
tolerated, if perhaps uneasily. Its patience gave out in October 1981.
Although no reason was given for suspending the journal's right to
publish, the suspension apparently stemmed from *Al-Azmina's* outspoken warnings against a second extension of the UAE's provisional
constitution, an attempt to pressure the rulers to complete the process
of writing and implementing a permanent constitution. With continuing differences between the rulers about the issue of the constitution
and with Shaikh Rashid, ruler of Dubai and prime minister of the
UAE, incapacitated by illness, Shaikh Zayed was not prepared to
allow the government to be embarrassed and perhaps weakened on
a sensitive issue by the press.

There is no very precise way to measure the impact of the press
on the public and the government, but its impact would appear to
be significant. This is evident in the degree to which the print media
have become an effective means of communication and mediation
between the public and the government, putting rulers in touch with
the people and their opinions. Officials from Shaikh Zayed on down
read newspapers closely, paying particular heed to what is written
on such matters as security and immigration issues. Moreover, a
government official has been appointed to monitor complaints and

proposals from the public. Letters and editorials in the press in fact bring responses from government. When, for example, the under-secretary of education in 1981 issued an edict permitting corporal punishment in the schools, the strong stand taken by the press against it led to the policy's revocation.

The press also plays an important role in a different way—by serving as a safety valve through which strong feelings can be vented. Thus, especially on those domestic and pan-Arab political issues that generate powerful emotions, the press is valuable in helping to let off steam. Doubtless, it is recognition of this aspect of the media's role that in large measure explains Shaikh Zayed's willingness to allow the print media to express opinions and take positions that are much out in front of the government's generally moderate policy stances.

Radio and television stations have been on the air for several years in the UAE. The range of programming is considerable, with a news and music format predominating in radio and a wide variety of programs available on television. Abu Dhabi, Dubai, and Ras al-Khaimah all have radio and television broadcasting, with Dubai's television signal reaching both sides of the Gulf and its UAE Radio heard as far away as Lebanon. Programming is about equally divided between English and Arabic, and one of Abu Dhabi's radio stations carries programs in Urdu as well. There is little evidence on which to base judgments about the significance of the electronic media, as television is not a political arena in the UAE. Most significant news is conveyed through the print media, which also appear to be far more important in molding public opinion. To some extent at least, television appears to have a negative cultural impact: It endangers the effort to keep the society's literary arts alive. Although the press can serve as a safety valve, television, with its graphic immediacy, may tend to do the opposite. Coverage of the Israeli invasion of Lebanon in 1982 and its destructive effects undoubtedly helped to intensify anti-Israeli and anti-U.S. opinion. It may be assumed that such actions as the Israeli raid on the Palestine Liberation Organization (PLO) headquarters in Tunis, with the killing of innocent bystanders and President Reagan's initial applause of the raid, help to reinforce anti-Israeli and anti-U.S. sentiment.

Arts and Entertainment: Traditional and Modern

Development of most art forms in what is now the UAE traditionally was limited by material poverty, isolation, and a generally conservative interpretation of the Islamic position on representation of nature in the visual arts. Religious conservatism also, of course, set strict limits for the performing arts. Nevertheless, as elsewhere in the Arab world, a tradition of oral poetry flourished, dealing more with bedouin courage and generosity than with religious themes. Religious ceremonies have always been important, an example being the religious recitations performed to commemorate the Prophet Muhammad's birth. In contrast to neighboring Saudi Arabia, where a more puritanical spirit flourished, music was a significant part of the area's culture, with drums and other simple instruments played on both religious and other occasions. Another typically bedouin ceremonial activity is a dance performed on festive occasions by prepubescent girls who swing their long hair from side to side in time to drums or voices. Some of these traditional performing arts survive, like the dance just noted, but increasingly, like traditional architecture, they are disappearing.

The traditional arts that remain most important are those that take the form of social rituals, accompanying the mundane activities of the people. The giving and receiving of hospitality in an area that even in the Arab world has always been noted for that aspect of its social behavior, remain a central part of the culture. One scholar recently pointed to the enormous significance of food and body rituals (the latter primarily encompassing women's dress and use of perfume and bodily adornments) within the general context of social and cultural values in the UAE. Those values reflect the aesthetic norms of Islam, helping to guide behavior in the way prescribed by Muhammad in the Quran and Hadith (traditions derived from what the Prophet did and said). Food and body rituals not only create aesthetic pleasure but serve an important purification function—physical and spiritual—and are meant to "reorder social experience."[24] Such rituals, then, are important in relating each person's activities to the purpose of the social group, emphasizing the primacy of the latter and channeling individual behavior within acceptable limits. This is an important factor in maintaining social stability in the face of rapid, dislocating change.

It is only in very recent years, in response to outside example and stimulus, that artistic activities of a contemporary nature have found a place in the UAE. Perhaps as a result of its earlier experience of modern education, Sharjah was the birthplace of a literary movement. To what extent this movement may flourish in the face of recreation that competes with the reading of short stories and poems is uncertain, especially in the wake of the suspension of *Al-Azmina al-Arabiyya*, a principal champion of Sharjah's writers.

In any event, a four-month-long theater workshop was first held in Sharjah in 1982 and was successful enough to be repeated. Attendance by some eleven amateur theater groups from within the UAE suggests the degree of interest in theater that has developed. Plays are being produced that depict familiar, folkloric themes. As such, theater is one example of artistic preservation of traditional themes or forms. Revival of the craft of traditional shipbuilding is another, and the striking new *suq* in Sharjah is a gratifying example of how imaginative city planning and architecture can create useful new public structures that convey a sense of continuity with the past. In Fujairah a number of ateliers produce handsome painted doors for the new houses being built there, thus readapting a traditional handicraft art in a useful and aesthetically pleasing way.

New forms of popular entertainment have become quickly and extensively established in the UAE. Many of these, however, are aimed more at the foreign than the indigenous population. Film theaters cater almost exclusively to audiences of expatriates from the subcontinent who watch a steady diet of romantic potboilers imported from India. Hotel shows and discos are also aimed principally at foreigners and draw only a small number of native Emirians. Moreover, such entertainment has recently been curtailed in the face of domestic religious pressure against it and to avoid providing additional ammunition for political attacks by the Khomeini regime in Iran. One Western entertainment innovation that has been widely embraced is dining out on fast food. Although initially appealing to a mostly non-Emirian clientele, burgers and shakes now seem to have caught on with the native population, including families at dinnertime and schoolchildren after classes. What deeper changes this may bring about in UAE society can probably not be discerned at this point, but a considerable alteration in the eating habits of the native population is being effected. This might eventually serve to undermine the closed private nature of family life and the traditional ritualized gustatory practices that serve to maintain and reinforce important social values.

Other kinds of entertainment would seem to reinforce, to some degree, traditional patterns of behavior. The ubiquitous television sets and stereos serve to keep families in their homes. What the impact of programming may be is uncertain: The range of tastes and ideas encountered is wide. Television entertainment offerings run from BBC productions of Jane Austen novels to religious commentaries. Foreign film and musical selections of nearly every kind reach the home audience in the form of video and audio cassette tapes.

Perhaps the most dramatic new development in the realm of recreation and entertainment is the popularity of sports. Traditionally, sports have been limited almost entirely to falconry—still a passionate diversion of Shaikh Zayed—and camel racing. Team sports, an alien, Western notion, were unknown until recently, and yet, as has been the case elsewhere in the Arabian Peninsula, soccer (known in the UAE by its European name, football) has been embraced with enormous enthusiasm. The government has made serious efforts to promote soccer, with considerable money invested initially in importing world-class expatriate players, then in training native players. The Higher Council of Youth and Sports, established as an autonomous body in 1980, determined that only UAE citizens would represent the country in international sports events after foreign players were phased out by the end of 1983. The sight of players exercising in the heat and humidity of a lower Gulf summer's day and the consistently large crowds in spacious stadiums in Abu Dhabi and elsewhere testify to the enormous popularity that soccer has achieved overnight. The 1984 Olympics, for which the Saudi and Qatari teams (though not the UAE team) qualified, served to affirm that Gulf Arabs can play on equal terms with some of the better national teams in the world.

This success has generated enormous national pride and may boost other sports already launched, including basketball, baseball, and volleyball. I was in the UAE in August 1981 when a young Dubayyan, Saeed Ahmed Saeed, won the world chess championship for players fourteen and under. He was received like a conquering hero on returning from Mexico City where the tournament was held, and his victory was cited as a "glittering landmark in the UAE's sports history."[25] One should guard against exaggerating the social or political importance of sports in the UAE. However, beyond altering the uses of leisure time—and, consequently, changing social behavior and values—this new phenomenon has the potential for strengthening a sense of national identity and pride.

The Position of Women in the UAE: Cautious Change

As is true elsewhere in the Arabian Peninsula, the persistence of traditional, Islam-based patterns of behavior has until recently kept women largely confined to the home and without any public role. However, women in Arab-Muslim society have always played a crucial role within the family, often exercising the real power—sometimes, indeed, tyranically—in the domestic domain. On occasion, women in ruling families have, therefore, been in a position to wield

influence over affairs of state. The mother of Shaikh Zayed made her
sons promise not to use violence in determining who among them
should rule the state of Abu Dhabi—a promise that was instrumental
in ending a long history of bloody succession struggles within the
ruling family. In Dubai the mother of the current Shaikh Rashid was
the most powerful personality in that shaikhdom until he reached
ruling age. Such occasions as these, however, have been rare and
have not—in a formal sense, at least—involved women leaving their
traditional sphere of activity.

Today, at first glance, not much has changed. Yet, a closer look
reveals that, both on the surface and in some more profound if quiet
ways, women's situation is changing. As a metaphor and a portent,
although most women are still cloaked in the formless black drapery
of the *abayah*, there has been a slow movement toward discarding
the *burqa*, the rigid face mask long worn in countries of the lower
Gulf.

The economic and social developments generated by oil wealth
have brought a more complex mode of life in which a wife educated
beyond traditional female skills is generally desired as an obvious
asset and a more desirable mate. Although the application of Islamic
law in marriage is unchallenged, other long-standing traditional
customs governing marriage are yielding to change.

Patriarchal authority is no longer so nearly absolute as it was.
Although the ties binding the extended family remain strong, living
patterns now reflect a move toward small nuclear families, a trend
made possible by the new money available for housing. A degree of
reaction against arranged marriages has led to the exercise of greater
choice by the marriage partners themselves. This, together with the
deferring of marriage by women who contemplate secondary or
university education, has led to more marriages between partners of
similar age and fewer of the unions common in the past between
young women and much older men. More emphasis is placed on
shared interests between spouses; greater leisure time means that
they tend to share more recreation together, and as a result, the
bonds between husbands and wives appear to be closer. Finally, the
phenomenon of the woman who is single by choice beyond the usual
age for marriage, something unheard of in this society in the past,
is no longer a curiosity.[26] The pace and scope of these changes vary
from emirate to emirate. Dubai and Sharjah have moved farther and
faster than Abu Dhabi.

Education is the most immediate cause of these changes. From
its inception, education for women has been popularly accepted and

with government encouragement of enrollment—plus the assurance of sexually segregated classrooms—most school-age girls are now being educated. The thirst for education among female students is evident from their academic accomplishments at the UAE National University, where they outperform their male counterparts, and from the enrollment of many married women in adult literacy classes. As women are widely educated they will inevitably play a more active role in society and the issue of women's participation in the economy will assume greater importance.

The changes being wrought in women's roles are occurring with the encouragement of government, not merely through government provision of educational opportunities for women but through its promotion of their more active involvement in society. This involvement encompasses social, artistic, recreational, and economic activities. The Ministry of Labor and Social Affairs has established centers in both urban and rural areas designed to promote women's "social development" through lectures and films on a variety of subjects, consultations with social workers, and visits to schools, hospitals, and modern institutions. Various women's organizations promote the intellectual, artistic, and social interests of women with the active support of Shaikha Fatima, wife of Shaikh Zayed. Television, radio, and the press carry serious discussions of women's affairs and two journals—*Zahra al-Khaleej* (Flower of the Gulf) and *Hiya* (She)—under female editors-in-chief are published for a solely female audience.

The number of women in the work force is not yet large, though it is growing. As of 1982, women accounted for 3.3 percent of the total work force (as compared to 6 percent in Saudi Arabia in the early 1980s and 43.7 percent in the United States in 1984), and their relative numbers were increasing.[27] Although Emirian women have entered several fields of work, most have been engaged in characteristically "female" occupations such as teaching, where segregation from men can be carefully maintained. Women students at the UAE National University continue to favor such fields as literature and education, but increasing numbers of female students are studying public administration and the sciences. These students will be seeking employment in traditionally male-dominated fields. Indeed, some small breaches in this domination have already been made. A few years ago the Abu Dhabi National Oil Company hired the first native female petroleum engineer, and the Ministry of Foreign Affairs accepted its first female employee. Other women have followed in the ministries of Labor and Social Affairs, Information, and Petroleum, and in public health services as well as in the police. The first woman to attain a senior ministerial position was Aisha al-Sayyar who, a few years ago, became an assistant deputy minister of education.[28]

In Abu Dhabi the Khaleej Commercial Bank, run by an entirely female staff, was established a few years ago and became a success. Generally, however, jobs in the private sector continue to be seen as unsuitable for women because they are likely to entail contact with men outside the immediate family. Women may head business organizations and delegate operational authority to men or invest, for example, in the bank mentioned above—a social outlet (i.e., a place where women can meet other women outside the home) as well as an economic opportunity for women. If women have thus far entered the economy in relatively small numbers and have remained largely segregated from men, it is interesting that they are nevertheless granted equal pay for equal work. Thus, in characteristic fashion, rapid and dramatic new developments are channeled through traditional cultural values. Women's entry into the professions seems already to have blurred the traditional sharp differentiation between the spheres of male and female activity. This is perhaps most immediately and visibly evident in broadcasting, where women have worked in a male context for a number of years. In dramatic contrast with neighboring Saudi Arabia, women are quite visible on local television as, for example, newscasters.

Impelled by the desire and the opportunity now available to experience greater self-fulfillment (rather than to satisfy economic need), women will continue to move into new fields and erode barriers of custom and usage that have limited their roles. Thus far, the government has committed itself to expand significantly the role that women can play in the country's development and to maintain the conservative, Islam-based values of UAE society. However, as more women are educated in a variety of professional fields and the model of the modern working woman becomes more common, it will be harder to reconcile these two goals. This potential dilemma could be heightened as efforts are made to reduce dependence on migrant workers, and trained native women are increasingly considered a source of skilled labor.

THE SCOPE OF CHANGE IN SOCIETY AND CULTURE— NOW AND IN THE FUTURE

Sudden wealth and the dramatic physical transformation of the UAE have in turn given rise to significant changes in the social and cultural dynamics of the country's population. Although basic values have not been challenged and by most standards—certainly those of contemporary U.S. society—UAE society remains deeply conservative, a potentially far-reaching process of transformation has been initiated. Its longer term implications are profound but not easily discerned.

In the short term the impact of Islamic revivalism and the pragmatic caution of the country's leadership will ensure a measured social change that does not directly challenge conservative values and the stability they engender. Moreover, certain developments in education, communications, and forms of recreation are promoting greater social and cultural integration, thereby contributing to social stability. During the next few years the structure and dynamics of UAE society will not be fundamentally altered. However, the forces of change already set in motion, in the longer run, may bring about a more extensive transformation. The sudden leap in rapid economic development and the generalized affluence that follows are producing a generation more dramatically removed from the circumstances of its parents' existence than in any other society. For most now in their teens or younger, there has been no direct experience of the impoverished, isolated existence that preceded oil wealth. Connections with the past are further weakened by the sudden exposure to other images and models of social behavior. Yet, beyond suggesting that a certain erosion or modification will occur in those basic cultural determinants that everywhere resist rapid alteration—family loyalties and religious norms—it is hard to project the extent and nature of change in the UAE of the future.

The values associated with the traditional, close-knit family and with the practice of conservative Islam are not theoretically incompatible with rapid economic development and the welfarism of super affluence, but their preservation will be much more difficult. What, then, lies ahead? Undoubtedly, over time, the changes already occurring in family living patterns will undercut the authority of heads of extended families, and there will be substantial weakening of tribal ties. Women will play important roles in parts of society from which they had always in the past been excluded. In short, there will probably be much greater social fluidity.

Although Islam has for so long provided the essential underpinning for the society and culture in this area that any real change in this respect is difficult to predict, some degree of secularization as has occurred in other Arab-Muslim countries long exposed to external non-Muslim influences would seem to be inevitable. (At the same time, of course, the current revival in Islam demonstrates its continued vitality and capacity for self-renewal.) What can with some certainty be anticipated is that as new ideas and perspectives gain further hold among younger elements of the population, society and culture will become more complex and ambivalent, leading eventually to changes not now easily envisioned. For some time to come, however, the essential nature of human behavior in the UAE and the norms and values that shape it will not be fundamentally altered.

NOTES

1. Frauke Heard-Bey points out that most earlier immigrants from the Persian coast were Sunnis. See *From Trucial States to United Arab Emirates* (London and New York: Longman, 1982), p. 133.

2. *MERI Report: United Arab Emirates* (London, Sydney, and Dover, N.H.: Croom Helm for the Middle East Research Institute, University of Pennsylvania, 1985), p. 6.

3. *The Economist* (April 25, 1981):44, 47.

4. Heard-Bey, *From Trucial States to Emirates*, pp. 77–80. Heard-Bey discusses the findings of Austrian anthropologist Walter Dostal, which have demystified the origins and identity of the Shihuh. Chapters 2 and 3 of *From Trucial States to Emirates* discuss in considerable detail the tribal dynamics of the UAE.

5. As of 1980 only Kuwait and Qatar had a slightly higher urban population among Gulf nations. See Paul Barker, "Boom Towns of the Gulf: The Rush to Service the Cities," *8 Days* (London), June 6, 1981, p. 13.

6. The British journalist Jonathan Raban provides perceptive glimpses of this in "Temporary People," Chapter 4 of his book *Arabia: A Journey Through the Labyrinth* (New York: Simon and Schuster, 1979).

7. Ibid., p. 143.

8. Ralph Magnus, "Societies and Societal Change in the Persian Gulf," in Alvin J. Cottrell et al., eds., *The Persian Gulf States: A General Survey* (Baltimore and London: Johns Hopkins University Press, 1980), p. 373.

9. Yves Schemeil, "Du Cadi au Caddie: Attitudes Envers la Modernisation dans les Pays du Golfe," [From Cadi to Caddie: Attitudes Toward Modernization in the Countries of the Gulf] in Paul Bonnenfant, ed., *La Péninsule Arabique d'Aujourd'hui* [The Arabian Peninsula Today] (Paris: Centre National de la Recherche Scientifique, 1982), p. 265.

10. "The Asian Labor Force Is a Fifth Column," *Al-Khaleej* (Sharjah), March 24, 1982, translated by Joint Publications Research Service (hereinafter referred to as JPRS).

11. "The Gulf: Survey," *The Economist* (December 13, 1980):40.

12. The rationale for emphasizing Asian labor was made by a member of the federal Parliament with striking candor: "We cannot deny that Asian labor brings its problems, but let us be frank: Arab labor brings in various political tendencies which have an affect on political stability." Quoted in an article by Ahmad Muhsin, "At a Lengthy Session of the Federal National Council, an Open Discussion of the Conditions of Foreign Workers—Ending

with a Secret Session," in *Al-Bayan* (Dubai), April 28, 1982, translated by JPRS.

13. *Al-Khaleej*, January 17, February 5, 1983, translated by JPRS.

14. Interview with author, August 27, 1981.

15. *Al-Bayan*, April 28, 1982, translated by JPRS.

16. Fred Arnold, "Asian Migrants Pump Oil Money Into Homelands," *Wall Street Journal*, March 5, 1984, p. 31. Also see Susannah Tarbush, "The New Nomads," *The Middle East*, no. 100 (February 1983):30. Tarbush credits a Pakistani psychiatrist with the coining of the expression "Dubai Syndrome" while Arnold suggests that its provenance is Korean.

17. Nasr el-Majali, "Brigadier General Abdallah Al-Sirri: 'We Will Not Allow the Manipulation of People's Security and Lives,'" *Al-Khaleej*, October 9, 1983, p. 9, translated by JPRS.

18. Sarah Graham Brown, "End of the Road," *The Middle East*, no. 112 (February 1984):18, 21.

19. The figures for schools and enrollment are from the 1982 "Human Rights Report for the UAE," prepared by the U.S. Department of State. Heard-Bey gives a figure of 108,840 for 1980-1981 student enrollment in all schools run by the UAE Ministry of Education and Youth, in *From Trucial States to Emirates*, p. 386. The figure for students abroad is cited in Trevor Mostyn, ed., *The UAE: A MEED Practical Guide* (London: Middle East Economic Digest, Ltd., 1982), p. 56. the same source notes (p. 56) that more than 14,000 students were enrolled in Education Ministry adult literacy programs and that nearly 26,000 were in 57 private schools, including those for children of expatriate workers.

20. "United Arab Emirates University" (in Arabic), pamphlet issued by the Office of Enrollment and Registration for the academic year 1980-1981 (no place or date of publication indicated); author's interview with Dr. Ezzedine Ibrahim, president of the UAE National University, August 31, 1981; and *An-Nahar Arab Report and Memo*, no. 10 (March 8, 1982):6–7.

21. The figures are from "United Arab Emirates University Student Directory, 1981-1982" (in Arabic), issued by the Office of Enrollment and Registration (no place or date of publication indicated), pp. 39–40.

22. Author's interview with Dr. Zuhdi al-Khatib, adviser to the Ministry of Education, September 1, 1981; The *UAE: A MEED Practical Guide*, p. 56; and author's interviews with members of staff and faculty of the UAE National University, August 31, 1981.

23. This and most of the observations and insights on the UAE press that follow are from interviews with writers and editors of newspapers in the UAE, August 25–26, 1981, and, especially, from discussions with Ibrahim al-Abed, director general of the UAE News Agency.

24. Aida S. Kanafani, *Aesthetics and Ritual in the United Arab Emirates* (Beirut: American University of Beirut Press, 1983), pp. 92, 106.

25. "Sporting Times for the U.A.E.," *Gulf News*, August 25, 1981.

26. Linda Usra Soffan, *The Women of the United Arab Emirates* (London and New York: Croom Helm and Barnes and Noble, 1980), pp. 21, 22, 23, 30, 44–46.

27. *Emirates News* (Abu Dhabi), June 28, 1982, p. 3.

28. Tahani al-Burtuqali, "Women in the Emirates Move Ahead with Great Speed," *Al-Siyasah* (Kuwait), May 7, 1982, translated by JPRS.

4

The Economy: Rush to Affluence

The UAE's emergence as a major oil-producing country has brought phenomenal affluence and one of the world's highest per capita incomes to its small number of citizens. However, before the discovery of oil most of the people of the lower Gulf enjoyed little prosperity. A mainly subsistence economy was based principally on date cultivation, a few other locally consumed vegetables and fruits, fishing, and the raising of livestock, mostly camels. The one significant resource of economic interest to the outside world was pearls, found in oysters growing at various depths in the Gulf. Both town dwellers along the coast and some of the bedouins of the interior manned the hundreds of ships that put out to the pearl banks, generally staying through the summer months.

The imposition of the British trucial system, and especially the 1853 Treaty of Perpetual Peace, provided a crucial degree of security for the pearlers. This, in addition to improved communications with India where the pearls were marketed, led to a significant expansion of the pearl trade through the nineteenth century and the first two decades of the twentieth. The export of pearls and of mother-of-pearl and the few auxiliary activities that it generated, such as shipbuilding, produced a significant amount of wealth.[1] Although only a relative handful of merchants grew wealthy, a very considerable part of the Trucial States population became dependent on the pearl trade for its livelihood. Thus, the rapid decline of that trade after the 1920s, due mainly to the worldwide economic depression and the introduction of Japanese cultured pearls, had a devastating effect on the lower Gulf economy.

The development of the pearl trade also created a group of merchant entrepreneurs, some of whom were able to utilize their skills in other businesses when the market for pearls collapsed. This was especially true in Dubai, which had already built up an entrepôt trade diverted from Iranian ports early in the century when high customs duties were imposed there. Dubai thus became a major Gulf port, enjoying a rather considerable pre-oil prosperity from export and re-export trade in contrast to its neighbors, whose economic eclipse was reversed only with the advent of oil income. Then and since much of Dubai's trade has been in gold.

THE OIL AND GAS SECTOR:
SINGLE RESOURCE AFFLUENCE

As noted in Chapter 2, oil exploration began in the 1930s and was seriously pursued after World War II in various parts of the then Trucial States. The first oil-related revenues were the exploration fees paid by prospecting companies to the rulers. Although by comparison with current oil income these sums seem trifling, they represented important new revenues for the emirate rulers who thereby enjoyed a source of wealth independent of the traditional merchant families. Thus, even before oil had been discovered and produced, its probable existence had generated important political consequences; the authority of the rulers was reinforced, and it was established that the state would henceforth be the principal economic actor.

The central place of oil in the economy of the UAE is evident: It accounts for approximately 90 percent of the country's income and about 95 percent of its trade earnings. The massive revenues of the hydrocarbon sector peaked at more than $20 billion in 1980, providing the total population of the UAE with a per capita income that exceeded $28,000 in 1980 and UAE citizens with a per capita income that is probably closer to $100,000. Despite the oil glut, per capita income in the UAE remains one of the highest in the world. (Per capita income in the United States, based on 1983 figures, is $11,675; for fiscal year 1981-1982, per capita income in Saudi Arabia was $18,344.) Production has been significant since the mid 1960s; it climbed to nearly 2 million barrels per day (mbpd) in 1976–1977 and settled at about 1.2 mbpd in 1983–1984. (see Figure 4.1). Thus, the UAE is a major oil-exporting country, accounting for more than 6 percent of OPEC's output. (In late 1984 the OPEC quota for the UAE was lowered to .95 mbpd, but it was not certain whether actual production fell to that mandated level.)

The UAE has proven reserves of about 32 billion barrels of oil (more than the United States including Alaska), and ongoing exploration continues to add to that figure. Thus, the UAE is assured of being an important producer for many years (at the current level of production, proven reserves would last for another seventy years). Of the total UAE reserves Abu Dhabi possesses by far the greatest

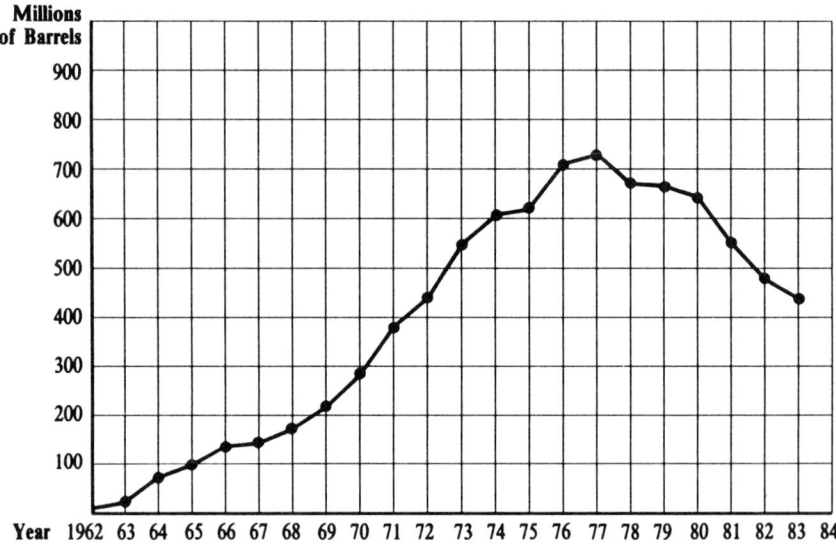

FIGURE 4.1 UAE oil production, 1962–1983 (based on Ragaei el-Mallakh, *Economic Development of the United Arab Emirates* [New York: St. Martin's Press, 1981], p. 103, and U.S. Department of State, "Economic Trends Report for the United Arab Emirates: July 1984," p. 2)

share—some 29 billion barrels. Dubai has 2.5 billion, and Sharjah and Ras al-Khaimah the remainder. Similarly, of total gas reserves, Abu Dhabi possesses the lion's share. With more than 2.5 trillion cubic meters/88.93 trillion cubic feet it has 2.8 percent of the world's total and is the fourth leading Middle East producer after Algeria, Saudi Arabia, and Iran. (At the present rate of production its gas reserves will last for about four hundred years.) Sharjah has gas reserves of more than .2 trillion cubic meters/7 trillion cubic feet, and Dubai is also endowed with significant reserves. As with oil, results of continuing exploration keep revising upward the figures for the amount of gas in the ground.

The rulers of the individual emirates retain control over their oil and gas resources, by provision of the UAE Constitution, and have pursued independent policies in exploiting them. As relative levels of reserves would suggest, Abu Dhabi accounts for the greatest share of UAE oil and gas production. However, that emirate reduced its production in the late 1970s, at a time of large surplus income (see Figure 4.2), as a conservation measure to maximize eventual production from its reserves. Then, as OPEC grappled with the impact of the oil glut, Abu Dhabi absorbed all the cuts imposed on UAE

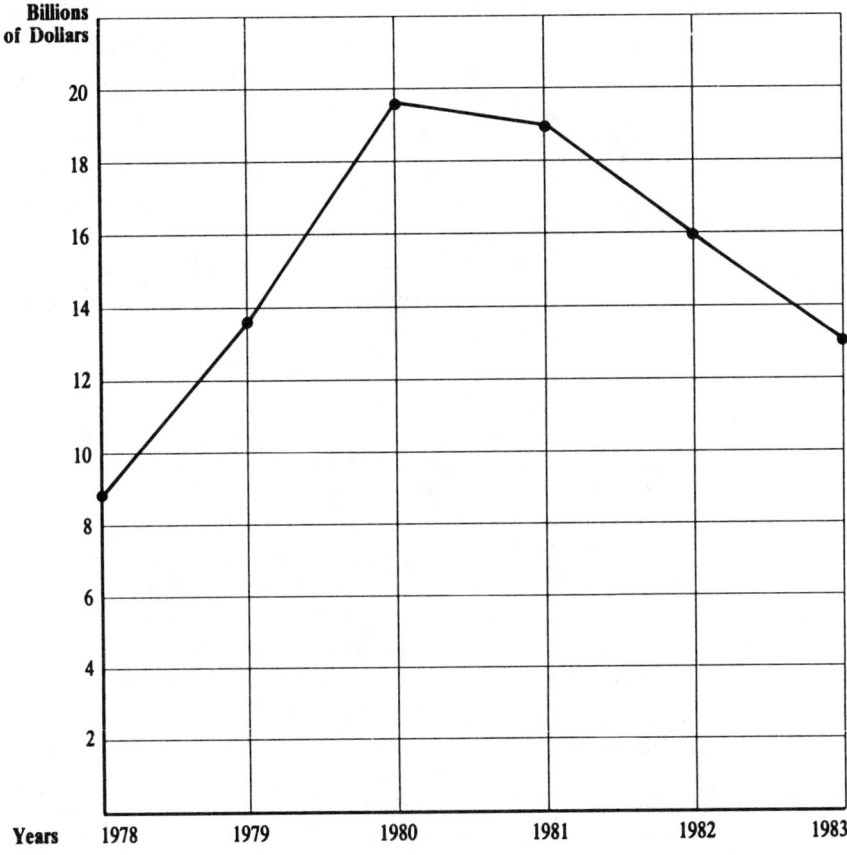

FIGURE 4.2 UAE oil and gas revenues, 1978–1983 (source: U.S. Department of State, "Economic Trends Report for the United Arab Emirates: July 1984," p. 2)

production (it is the only emirate subject to OPEC quotas) while Dubai and Sharjah continued to produce at their preferred levels.

Although at one time Abu Dhabi alone produced 1.7 mbpd, by early 1983 its production had sunk to well under half that amount, subsequently rebounding to approximately 800,000 barrels per day (bpd). Dubai has held steady at around 350,000 bpd and Sharjah close to 70,000 bpd, mostly in the form of condensate. Thus, about two-thirds of the UAE's income from oil and gas exports, currently amounting to approximately $13 billion, goes to Abu Dhabi. Sharjah's income from fields in the area of Abu Musa Island is shared with Umm al-Qaiwain and Ajman (which have 20 percent and 10 percent shares respectively) because both have claims to the island and the territorial waters. Sharjah, which itself shares the revenue from this offshore production with Iran, following the latter's seizure of the island in 1971, was forced in the summer of 1984 to suspend oil exploration in those waters because of Iran's sensitivities regarding its apparent buildup of military facilities on the island.[2] In late 1983 Ras al-Khaimah's first commercial oil discovery was made offshore, with initial production in early 1984 at 6,000 bpd, raised to 10,000 bpd after the addition of a second producing well. The scope of Ras al-Khaimah's reserves and level of sustainable production have yet to be determined, but will presumably be modest, though of great significance for that emirate.

Policymaking

The UAE, aside from Nigeria, is the only OPEC state where Western companies can still be equity-holders in a concession. At the same time, those companies are obligated to share in the necessary investment in operations. Company-government relations have generally been positive since the mid-1960s as both joined in developing the country's hydrocarbon resources.

Policies regulating development of oil and gas vary from one emirate to another. Outside of Abu Dhabi the rulers generally deal directly with companies in negotiating and administering concessions. Just before independence in November 1971, Abu Dhabi established a state corporation, the Abu Dhabi National Oil Company (ADNOC), which has come to dominate that emirate's oil and gas sector. ADNOC engages in the oil business at all levels, with twenty-four subsidiaries including a refinery and tanker fleet. The two main operating companies, the Abu Dhabi Company for Onshore Oil Operations (ADCO) and Abu Dhabi Marine Areas Operating Company (ADMA-Opco), are owned by ADNOC (60 percent) and by private European and U.S. companies (40 percent). Such joint concessions are run by committees of both government and company representatives, and the companies' profit reflects the difference between the official selling price of the equity-holders' crude oil entitlement and the production cost plus tax on posted prices and a royalty payment.

Abu Dhabi has relied on an able team of Algerians to run ADNOC. Although the Algerians' influence, which has helped to keep the foreign oil companies in check, has been considerable, all ADNOC management decisions are reviewed by the Abu Dhabi Executive Council chaired by Abu Dhabi Crown Prince Shaikh Khalifa bin Zayed. A U.S. consulting firm then scrutinizes ADNOC's policy for the council. The growing trend toward promoting the role of local business establishments, discussed later in this chapter, has led Abu Dhabi (though not the other emirates) to limit bidding on government tenders, including those in the oil and gas sector, to companies run by UAE nationals.[3] However, the basic goal of developing eventual self-reliance in managing the country's oil and gas operations argues for continuing good relations with the companies from which technical and managerial expertise can be learned. The outlook, then, is for a moderate and generally friendly policy toward outside private oil interests that also carefully safeguards the nation's single great resource and promotes its optimum development.

Strategies for Future Development

Looking ahead from the 1980s, there are several dimensions to the UAE's strategy for maximizing the future development potential of its hydrocarbon resources. Despite the present cutbacks in production due to the worldwide oil glut, the search for new oil and gas reserves continues to be pressed vigorously using the most sophisticated, computer-based seismic exploration techniques. This has resulted in recent major new finds in Dubai and Sharjah as well as Ras al-Khaimah's first commercially viable discovery, as noted above. Among the remaining oil havenots, Umm al-Qaiwan is encouraged by a recent seismic survey whose results led a consortium of U.S. firms to begin exploratory drilling in December 1984. Virtually all of Dubai is now being explored while more companies have been attracted to Sharjah and Ras al-Khaimah as well. The concern of each emirate, especially Dubai, has been to maximize current production. Abu Dhabi, by contrast, is at least as concerned with conservation and therefore with sustaining the source of its wealth for as long as possible. While making major efforts through ADNOC to add to its recoverable reserves, Abu Dhabi also uses current field management technology to prolong the life of existing fields of oil and gas. Abu Dhabi thus seeks to ensure that it will remain a major oil and gas producer at least to the middle of the next century.

Another strategy for hydrocarbon development is the increased emphasis on gas—its discovery, field maintenance, and various forms of utilization. "Associated gas," a byproduct with petroleum that was formerly flared off, is now exported (almost exclusively to Japan) or used locally. A major problem resulting from lowered oil production is that the level of associated-gas production falls with it, a situation that has forced Abu Dhabi to draw on "cap" gas in another field, thereby risking a decline in eventual oil recovery. Development of deep, "nonassociated gas" is now being pressed and will help to alleviate the current shortage and promote independence of oil production levels.

Abu Dhabi has recently completed its Thamama C project to gather nonassociated gas already being supplied to some power stations; the gas will also fuel the refinery and power and desalination plants in the Ruwais industrial zone as well as provide feedstock for the hydrocracker and fertilizer plants there. Abu Dhabi is presently the Gulf's only producer of liquified natural gas (LNG); it also produces liquified petrloeum gas (LPG) along with Dubai. Sharjah is now constructing an LPG facility. An expanded gas recovery system in Dubai provides most of the fuel needs for Dubai Aluminum Company, that emirate's aluminum-producing company, and may eventually power all new industries at the Jebel Ali industrial zone. In Sharjah a major gas distribution project is underway to run power stations and service industrial consumers in the northern emirates. Given the size of the UAE's reserves, gas is certain to play an increasingly important role both in fueling the local economy and providing export income.

Finally, like its Gulf Arab neighbors, the UAE is moving in a direction called downstream in petroleum parlance—away from being simply a crude oil producer and exporter. Abu Dhabi now processes about one-fourth of its oil production, some 200,000 bpd, though virtually all refined products are consumed locally. (Not very long ago even gasoline for local use had to be brought in from outside.) However, Abu Dhabi has already contracted to export part of the output from its fertilizer plant. The emirate of Ajman plans to set up a refinery purchased secondhand from the United Kingdom to refine Saudi or Abu Dhabi crude for export mainly to Gulf countries. Increasingly, though, the UAE and the other Gulf states will be boosting the export of petrochemicals to European, U.S., and Japanese markets.

The UAE and OPEC

The UAE belongs both to the nine-member Organization of Arab Petroleum Exporting Countries (OAPEC) as well as to the better-known thirteen-member Organization of Petroleum Exporting Countries (OPEC). It has played a significant role in the affairs of each: OAPEC is involved primarily in promoting regional, oil-related projects and OPEC in overseeing the price and production levels of its members. The UAE's Minister of Petroleum Affairs, Dr. Mana Said al-Otaiba, is chairman of OPEC's Ministerial Monitoring Committee and, thus, closely involved in the committee's critical efforts to maintain discipline in the members' ranks in the face of a prolonged oil glut.

With its Gulf Arab neighbors, the UAE has generally been one of the moderates in OPEC, reflecting an interest in promoting a stable hydrocarbon export market over the long term. In particular, the UAE has tended to coordinate its oil policy closely with that of Saudi Arabia. Both nations have high per capita incomes, large oil reserves (absolutely and in relation to production), and, in recent years, have accumulated large financial surpluses. Each has cut back very heavily on production with the lowering of OPEC quotas. The March 1982 OPEC decision to establish a 17.5 mbpd production limit required that the UAE lower its production by 400,000 bpd, a cut that, as noted earlier, had to be absorbed by Abu Dhabi, though reports that UAE production has continued above its quota have persisted since then. In early 1983 Dr. al-Otaiba's threat to raise UAE production dramatically was part of the Gulf Arab states' strategy to pressure Iran, Nigeria, and other OPEC rivals to stop encroaching on their market shares. After vowing earlier to hold the line on prices, he helped engineer OPEC's first-ever price cut at the October 1983 OPEC meeting: The $34 dollar per barrel benchmark price was lowered to $29.

Despite further production quota cuts in November 1984, which reduced the total OPEC output to 16 mbpd, the soft (i.e., buyer's) market continued, and the UAE began almost immediately to offer discounts to producing companies operating its fields. At the December 1984 OPEC meeting Dr. al-Otaiba, a poet as well as a technocrat, inscribed the following verse:

> After the days of luxury,
>   we have become
> A lamb in the midst of the jungle.
> Like a gang, the wolves of the market
> Swirl around us.[4]

With its small population, large financial reserves, and sizable potential oil production, the UAE is better able to weather the crisis than most other OPEC producers and remains in a position to play a major role in OPEC during the most critical phase in that organization's existence. However, there will be a period of stress that tests the capability of the OPEC moderates to work together.

In late 1984–early 1985 the previous harmony and cooperation that characterized relations among Dr. al-Otaiba and the oil ministers of Saudi Arabia and Kuwait gave way to strains brought on by continued depressed world oil demand. The UAE was not happy with the lowered production quota assigned to it and was particularly upset about the Saudi-Kuwaiti refusal to raise the price of heavy crude oil to reflect heavy crude's enhanced desirability vis-à-vis light crude on the world market. (By the mid-1980s, with many refineries modified to process the heavier oils that form a large part of Saudi and Kuwaiti production, producers of the formerly more desirable light oil, like the UAE, were at a disadvantage.) The UAE found itself siding with other producers of lighter crudes, such as Libya and Algeria, against its erstwhile close allies in OPEC. Although this probably should not be seen as betokening a permanent or even long-term shift in relations between OPEC states, it has led to considerable bitterness of feeling among old friends. There was an attempt by the Saudi and Kuwaiti oil ministers in December 1984 to do away with the production quota committee that Dr. al-Otaiba has long headed in OPEC. Relations are likely to remain strained until some improvement in world oil demand occurs.

INFRASTRUCTURE

The development needs of the UAE combined with the availability of enormous oil revenues, which were massively boosted by the oil price rises of 1974 and 1979, generated a dramatic surge in construction in the early 1980s. By 1982-1983 the general construction boom had given way to a slump brought on by the oil glut. However, the essential work of providing the physical infrastructure necessary for the nations' economic development had by then been largely completed (projects since cancelled or deferred are not of prime importance).

The growth in physical infrastructure has been matched by the increase in communciations. Communications have in a short span of time been revolutionized, a fact of great political as well as economic importance because they serve to knit together the separate, frequently contentious emirates. As noted earlier, various parts of the country have been linked by a first-class road system. Abu Dhabi, Dubai, Sharjah, and Ras al-Khaimah all have airports that service both international and domestic flights. This overbuilding, prompted by interemirate rivalry, has left the latter two facilities underutilized. Abu Dhabi, on the other hand, recently opened a new, large civilian airport to handle its traffic. Dubai, with the busiest airport in the Gulf, is upgrading its facilities in a scheme to be completed in 1986. Several major, modern seaports have come into being since UAE independence. Dubai city had the largest seaport by far before the oil boom and has maintained its preeminence with a continuing expansion of Port Rashid, adjacent to the city of Dubai, and the various facilities that service shipping including the Gulf's biggest shipyard, the Dubai drydock (expanded in 1978). Regarded by many as senseless duplication of Bahrain's similar facility, it began to do a brisk business in 1983, justifying its creation. About 20 miles to the west, Dubai is creating a vast second port to serve its new industrial and free-trade zone at Jebel Ali. At the city of Abu Dhabi, where in the late 1960s imported goods were dumped from lighters onto the beach, a large port has been created. At Jebel Dhanna, about 160 miles west of Abu Dhabi city, is the emirate's main oil terminal, and, just to its east, extensive port facilities are being provided for the built-from-scratch industrial city of Ruwais.

Several smaller ports also have also assumed a degree of importance. On the Gulf, Sharjah features roll-on, roll-off facilities, and Khor Fakkan, in the emirate's Gulf of Oman enclave, has become a significant container port. The development of Khor Fakkan and of Fujairah's port a few miles to the south has assumed potential strategic importance with the threat of spillover by the Iran-Iraq war into the Gulf. Presently, a project is being launched to build an oil pipeline across the country, exiting at Fujairah. Finally, it should be noted that a superb system of telecommunications links the emirates with each other and the rest of the world.

Construction of the other facilities and amenities for promoting economic development has been equally dramatic. First-class hotels are found throughout the country, and the expansion of office and exhibition space has been well designed to meet the needs of the business community. In the latter connection Shaikh Rashid's much criticized construction of the Dubai International Trade Center, the tallest building in the Arab world, sited outside Dubai city proper, has proven, like his other bold gambles, to be a brilliant success.

The development of social infrastructure, discussed at some length in Chapter 3, has also been emphasized. A far-reaching social welfare system has provided housing on generous terms and free health care and education (full benefits are available only to citizens, however). In addition, fed increasingly by domestic food production, the UAE's population enjoys one of the highest nutrition levels in the developing world. The essential problem remains the effective training and mobilization of indigenous human resources. The lack of effective national training programs addressed to all areas of the economy and the failure to place graduates in the appropriate jobs remain significant shortcomings as does the still high dropout rate in elementary and high schools. All of these factors ensure critical dependence on imported skills for the foreseeable future.

ECONOMIC DIVERSIFICATION

Given the scarcity of other resources it is inevitable that the hydrocarbon sector will continue to dominate the UAE's economy in the near future. However, the country has clearly recognized the need for economic diversification. Progress has been made in freeing the UAE economy from dependence on the export of crude oil and gas toward production and export of refined products and the creation of industries based on hydrocarbon feedstocks. Another step in this process is to create industries that can take advantage of the availability of cheap energy. Finally, some forms of industrial and other economic activity independent of the hydrocarbon sector are being developed. In all of this the constraints of a very small domestic market are obvious as is the need to emphasize capital-intensive projects in the absence of sufficient indigenous skilled labor.

As the previously noted duplication of infrastructure projects among the emirates would suggest, there has been a lack of coordinated strategy to promote diversified industrial development. Only Abu Dhabi, beginning in 1968, produced development plans prior to 1981 when the federal government adopted a five-year plan to promote a more unified approach. Still, it should be kept in mind that the individual emirates retain their separate budgets and that Abu Dhabi's remains larger than that of the UAE. By the terms of a 1980 agreement, both Abu Dhabi and Dubai are to give equal proportions of their oil revenues to the federal budget, thereby generating development throughout the federation, especially in the poorer emirates. In practice, Abu Dhabi gives a greater relative share, in 1982 providing more than 82 percent of the total UAE budget. In large measure, industries being developed or contemplated are designed to provide import substitutes, though generation of nonhydrocarbon exports is also envisioned.

In the wealthy emirates of Abu Dhabi and Dubai principal emphasis has been on industries spun off from the hydrocarbon sector. The former, for example, has established plants for the manufacture of ammonia, sulfur, and fertilizer and has plans at the Ruwais industrial complex for an iron and steel works. Abu Dhabi has also developed its own cement manufacturing capacity and has constructed flour mills aimed at supplying the UAE's domestic requirements. At Dubai's Jebel Ali complex the Dubai Aluminum Company (DUBAL), run by natural gas from the Dubai Gas Company (DUGAS), produces approximately 140,000 tons of aluminum annually. Japan is the chief customer, with significant production going also to other Gulf countries. DUBAL uses heat from its smelter to provide Dubai city with desalted water and has spun off associated chemical industries using solar evaporation to produce crude salts. Another Jebel Ali project is Dubai Cables (DUCAL), which exports technically advanced power cables.

Sharjah, with both its own oil earnings and some federal funds for investment in development, has looked largely to the development of hydrocarbon-based industries. However, the Sharjah Economic Development Corporation (SHEDCO) has recently established as its first plant a company that manufactures large spiral pipe (used for oil pipelines). Ajman has a steel fabrication plant and ship repair yard, and Ras al-Khaimah mines and exports marble, limestone, stone aggregate, and other materials used in construction. Each of these emirates, as well as Umm al-Qaiwain, manufactures cement, with a danger now of overproduction that could be alleviated with the upsurge of Gulf area construction following a winding down of the Iran-Iraq war. Fujairah, with the construction of an oil pipeline across its territory to the Gulf of Oman, anticipates creation of a local petrochemicals industry in the near future. In the meantime it is developing a natural resource in large supply—the minerals at hand in the Hajar Mountains, which include chrome, iron, copper, and uranium (the metallic ores are found in Ajman as well). In addition to a cement plant, there are companies manufacturing ceramic tile, finished marble, and rockwool insulation.

Tourism offers one further avenue of economic diversification. Until recently there was no tourist industry apart from hotel and other facilities to serve citizens and foreigners in the country for business or official reasons. Now efforts are being made to attract part of the international tourist trade. Since 1981, package tours covering several of the emirates have been available. Sharjah, utilizing some of its overbuilt hotel space, is attracting thousands of Europeans annually. Umm al-Qaiwain, with miles of excellent beaches, is hoping that tourism will bring it significant added income. Given the country's proximity to Europe, its pleasant winter weather, and its modern amenities, the UAE should be able to exploit further its tourist potential, though in a much more modest way than the major established vacationing sites given the country's size and lack of dramatic or well-known attractions.

AGRICULTURE

Thanks to sizable capital inputs made possible by oil revenues, UAE agricultural production has experienced a remarkable expansion. According to one set of figures, overall food production increased by 200 percent in the decade following independence, vegetable pro-

Table 4.1. Selected UAE Agricultural Production

	1977	1981
Field crops	23,000 tons	123,000 tons
Fruits	38,000 tons	146,000 tons
Vegetables	40,000 tons	160,000 tons
Poultry	600 tons	2,500 tons
Eggs	25 million	53 million

Source: Department of State airgram, "January 1985 Agri-business Trade Mission," US Embassy in Abu Dhabi, March 27, 1984, p. 2.

duction alone rose by 62 percent per annum, and cultivated land expanded by 500 percent. Table 4.1 illustrates the growth of production in selected areas.

The federal government's commitment to promoting the nation's agriculture is evident in its annual budgetary allotment, now close to $50 million a year. Further investment is reflected in the budgets of individual emirates. In terms of the UAE's overall development this emphasis makes sense as it channels assistance to the poor northern emirates where agriculture is most feasible. More importantly, though, it signals the government's commitment to achieving security in its food supply through local production of most if not all basic foodstuffs. The UAE may soon achieve self-sufficiency in poultry and vegetables, most fruits, and, possibly, fish production. Indeed, surpluses of some crops are now exported to neighboring countries, though agriculture is certainly not considered a source of foreign exchange. The country is uneasy about dependence on lifelines (i.e., imported food) running through the troubled waters of the Gulf and, like its neighbor Saudi Arabia, has taken a leaf from the oil consumers who have sought security of energy supplies and applied the lesson to food.

Policy Goals

The government has undertaken a variety of initiatives to promote its agricultural policy goals. The Digdaga scheme in Ras al-Khaimah, whose relatively more favorable climate has made it the most significant emirate in agriculture, is the oldest and among the most important government experimental projects. There, on 380 acres belonging to

The Arid and Semi-arid Lands Research Center on Sadiyat Island, Abu Dhabi. Cucumbers (shown here) and other vegetables are grown under carefully controlled conditions. Unit costs are uneconomically high for the products of this experimental facility, but valuable lessons for future agricultural developments are learned.

the Agricultural Trials Station, many varieties of fruits and vegetables are grown, and encouraging work has been done to adapt livestock, including dairy cattle, to the local conditions, feeding them with locally produced fodder. There are other dairy farms in Abu Dhabi (at al-Ain), Umm al-Qaiwan, and Dubai; together they supply a significant part of the population with fresh milk. With the establishment of a large poultry farm in Fujairah early in 1985, total UAE production of poultry was expected to meet 40 percent of demand and egg production to satisfy 70 percent.[5] Several agricultural projects employ sophisticated, state-of-the-art technology. For more than a decade the Sadiyat Island Arid and Semi-arid Lands Research Center, set up with the assistance of specialists from the University of Arizona, has produced a variety of fruits and vegetables in an artificially controlled environment. Though the yield per acre is phenomenal, the cost appears too great to make that kind of production commercially feasible on a large scale. Knowledge gained, however, will have relevance for other developments. In al-Ain, traditionally Abu Dhabi's principal agricultural area, a desert development station is using

Drying nets in Umm al-Qaiwain. This scene suggests the potential that exists in the UAE for promoting a major fishing industry. Its development has been difficult, however, because better paying positions in the UAE's labor-short economy bid away workers.

advanced methods of countering the porosity of sandy desert soil to make vegetable cultivation feasible. Research centers have been established in several other locales as well where government and FAO experiments are determining which crops can most effectively be grown in particular areas.

With the country's past closely linked to the sea, fishing has been a significant economic activity. In the decades immediately before the oil boom fish were a significant export item. Both coasts have rich potential to be exploited; the Gulf of Oman's potential is somewhat greater. (It remains to be seen how much damage the continuing oil spill initiated in 1983 will cause in the Gulf.) The government is promoting efforts to develop a modern fishing industry, setting up coastal fish farms, and carrying out research on such matters as the use of mangrove swamps as fish habitats.

The Ministry of Agriculture and Fisheries is committed to developing both the human and technical resources required to create a modern agricultural base. Each of the four agricultural areas into which the country is divided maintains extension centers that provide technical services and, through specialists, provide expert advice to farmers. More than 200 demonstration farms are also designed to improve farming techniques.[6] In 1981 an agricultural college was created at the UAE National University in al-Ain to expand the nation's cadre of professional agronomists. Appropriate equipment, scientific expertise, and managerial practices are sought from various sources, but the United States plays a key role. In September-October 1984 H. E. Saeed al-Ragabani, minister of agriculture and fisheries, visited the United States with several aides, the first time that a UAE cabinet officer had done so. Mettings with Secretary of Agriculture Block and other U.S. Department of Agriculture (USDA) officials as well as with agricultural specialists in Arizona and California touched on numerous aspects of crop and livestock production and on forms of government support to farmers. (I had the privilege of helping to arrange the minister's appointments during his visit, which was sponsored by the U.S. Information Agency.)

Despite the degree of official commitment to developing the UAE's agricultural resources and the very considerable success already achieved, there are still major constraints to overcome. The average size of a UAE farm is very small for efficient operation. Price fluctuations and the threat thereof are also inhibiting. Further, emirate-federal coordination is not always sufficient, transportation costs remain high, and marketing techniques remain ineffective. Even if these obstacles are surmounted, there remains a severe twofold limitation—a lack of water and of indigenous labor.

Currently, the availability of water in various parts of the desert is helping to make possible an ambitious afforestation program in Abu Dhabi, paralleled by similar but more modest efforts in Dubai and Sharjah. Afforestation is intended to reduce soil erosion and protect crops from wind and sand. Some have theorized that afforestation also stimulates increased rainfall such as formerly supported greater vegetation. In Abu Dhabi municipality a remarkable "greening" has occurred during the past few years with palms, acacias, bougainvillea, hibiscus, and various other flowering plants now gracing road dividers, roundabouts (rotaries), and the city's numerous parks.

The afforestation program, one that is particularly close to the heart of Shaikh Zayed, is much in evidence all the way from Abu Dhabi to al-Ain. Acacia and eucalyptus trees, all irrigated daily (some by filtered sewage water), line the route. In addition, the highway from al-Ain to Dubai is lined with trees, and various other desert locations where shallow aquifers can be tapped are being planted with tree seedlings. As of late 1981 a total of about 4 million trees, including those within the Abu Dhabi municipality, had been planted.

The greening of Abu Dhabi. An area of irrigated acacia seedlings between the city of Abu Dhabi and al-Ain is part of an ambitious effort to convert much of the desert to forested land. The young trees are sustained by water drawn up from a shallow aquifer and distributed by the black plastic pipes visible in the foreground.

A number of companies are carrying out afforestation projects under contract to the Abu Dhabi government. In August 1981 I had an opportunity to visit one such project, Bu Deeb, located north of the Abu Dhabi—al-Ain highway where a major aquifer runs north-south for some miles. Here 84,000 acacia seedlings covering an area of .6 x 3 miles are irrigated daily with 2–3 gallons of water each, drawn from 9 open pit wells. In 1981 it cost 120 dirhams (about $32) to plant and maintain each seedling for two years.

In the UAE's harsh climate rainfed agriculture is impossible. Except for the 2 percent or so of the agricultural water supply that comes through the ancient, underground *falaj* system from mountain run-off, all water used for growing crops comes from wells. (Sadiyat Island's experimental work is done with desalted water, a source not economically feasible for commercial agriculture, and some afforestation work is carried out with retreated sewage.) Agriculture uses nearly three-fourths of the UAE's total water supply—more than four times as much as industry—and is depleting the country's aquifers at an alarming rate and causing severe increases in salinity in some areas. The extraordinary rains of February–March 1982, which replenished the aquifers at one stroke, were undoubtedly an aberration unlikely to recur for many years. Further use of dams to improve water storage, application of the most efficient irrigation techniques, and implementation of sophisticated crop production under plastic coverings may alleviate if not solve the problem. But even if the water problem is met, the continuing movement of UAE citizens out of the agricultural sector means increasing reliance on relatively unskilled immigrant labor, thereby jeopardizing the goals of more efficient modernized agriculture and lessened dependence on foreign workers.[7] Whether the complex and daunting challenge of self-sufficient security in food production can be fully met, the effort to achieve it will yield economic benefits and, by involving a broad national effort, should strengthen political unity as well.

THE BUSINESS AND FINANCIAL SECTORS

The flood of oil revenues during the past few years has enormously expanded the number and prominence of business enterprises in the wealthy emirates. Although the oil sector is government-controlled, private enterprise is vigorously encouraged in a number of ways. Moreover, as noted earlier, the lines between the private and public sectors are crossed and blurred more easily than in most Western countries. The primary occupation of most of the more enterprising citizens of the UAE is business.

Dubai had a head start in developing an important commercial sector well before the advent of oil wealth because of its development as a major regional entrepôt in the earlier decades of this century. (Many considerable fortunes were made through gold smuggling.) Merchant families from the Iranian side of the Gulf have played a prominent role in Dubai; many of them have been established there for several generations. The ruling Maktum family's own strong commercial predilections have to the present ensured maintenance of a climate favorable to trade, commerce, and other business interests. With the injection of oil income, most of the traditional merchant enterprises successfully adapted to changing circumstances. Families like the Galadaris, Ghurairs, and Futtaims have built considerable business empires with acumen, sophistication, and boldness.

Abu Dhabi's business community, by contrast, is essentially a postoil boom phenomenon and, therefore, lacks the roots, scope, and energy of its Dubai counterpart. Prominent families were able to launch themselves in business, relying in large measure on expatriate managers to carry on the daily affairs of their enterprises. With acquired experience these firms are now becoming more aggressive and sophisticated, and, by virtue of its much greater oil wealth, Abu Dhabi has come to represent the largest business market in the Emirates. In Abu Dhabi, Dubai, and, to a lesser extent, elsewhere in the UAE, a great many small and medium retail establishments are the province of expatriates, especially Indians and Pakistanis.

THE CLIMATE FOR FOREIGN BUSINESS AND INVESTMENT

Foreign exchange and business investment in the UAE continue to be generally welcome and protected because the governing authorities favor private enterprise and the country continues to depend on foreign manufactures as well as technological and professional expertise from abroad. There are neither foreign exchange controls nor laws directly regulating foreign investment, and no such legislation is anticipated. Although some income tax laws exist at the emirate level, most foreign businesses are not subject to such taxation. Moreover, no limitation has been imposed on repatriation of profits.

However, since 1979, two developments have altered the way in which foreign business activity is conducted in the UAE: (1) implementation of emirate and federal regulations governing participation by UAE nationals in business enterprises and (2) a general movement toward more regulation in codified form at the federal level. Although application of federal regulations may not override all discrepancies in existing emirate regulations, the earlier practice of ad hoc arrangements between emirate rulers and foreign businesses is past.

The Federal Companies Law (also referred to as the Commercial Companies Law), signed by UAE President Shaikh Zayed, and published in the *Official Gazette* in April 1984, is the capstone of the process of regulating the manner in which foreign businesses are conducted. It reaffirms the provision of earlier regulations stipulating that any company established in the UAE must have at least 51 percent of its equity capital held by UAE citizens. If a company is represented by a branch office in the UAE, that office must be sponsored by a local citizen. The same law has the effect of making the limited liability form of company the only practical way for most foreign businesses to enter into a joint venture, replacing the partnership arrangement that had hitherto prevailed. Although all the implications of the new law are not yet clear, all companies operating in the UAE will henceforth be subject to a much greater amount of detailed regulation.[8] The complexities of implementing the new regulations led the government to defer doing so from the date originally set—July 1, 1984—to January 1, 1985, then to December 31, 1985. At the end of 1985, however, it was anticipated that implementation of the Federal Companies Law would be deferred for yet another six months.

Codification of regulations governing foreign business operations in the UAE should be helpful in creating greater certainty as to the relevant laws, but there remains some concern about how far changes reflected in the new regulations will go. For example, in October 1984 the UAE's Federation of Chambers of Commerce and Industry proposed that foreign-owned companies be compelled to reinvest part of their profits in local enterprises. Calls for taxes and other restrictions on foreign companies are anticipated, and, although none of these measures is likely to be effected soon, they all suggest future complications brought about by the government emphasis on promoting the role of local companies.[9] There remains further uncertainty about how the UAE's courts will actually interpret and apply legislation. Despite the fact that the country's legal system is based on Islamic law—the Sharia—the system incorporates, directly and indirectly, elements of European law. Generally accepted international practice in commercial law is usually adhered to and, by and large, is in harmony with the pertinent principles of the Sharia. However, despite the move toward greater regulation at the federal level, individual emirates differ significantly in their customary application of federal laws. Also, the UAE Sharia courts continue to rely largely on judges from other Arab countries who tend to act with great independence in adjudicating commercial disputes. A certain degree of arbitrariness implied in the above circumstances, combined with the move to promote local business interests, leads some Western observers to perceive bias against outsiders.[10] Although there may be an element of truth in this, the major problem introduced by the recent legal changes is confusion as foreign-owned businesses adjust to a new system of regulation that is itself not yet fully in place. It is reasonable to assume that the practical recognition of the UAE's economic development needs will compel continued and significant participation of foreign companies on reasonable terms.

Banking Reforms

The reforms enacted in response to problems in the banking sector are simpler, more obvious, and viewed almost universally as necessary and beneficial. Foreign banks flocked to the UAE in the 1970s; there was a total of 347 bank branches, 222 belonging to foreign banks, by the end of the decade. However, the expansion of the banking sector became excessive, as was apparent in 1977 when overextension of credit fueled a building boom that produced more new construction than was needed, and borrowers had trouble repaying loans. That banking crisis led the UAE Currency Board, in the same year, to place a moratorium on establishment of new offices by foreign banks, and in 1981 its more powerful successor, the Central Bank, dictated the closure of 89 such branches and imposed a limit of 8 branches per bank. Thus, a policy parallel to those policies pursued in regard to other kinds of foreign business is being implemented in the financial sector. Local banks dominate the UAE scene, led by the National Bank of Abu Dhabi, or NBAD (one of the top ten Arab banks), a merchant banking branch of the Abu Dhabi Investment Authority, which handles the Abu Dhabi government's long-term investments. NBAD is typical of the hybrid private/public enterprise institutions in the UAE and the Gulf generally. Curiously, there is a shortage of liquidity in the UAE because the government invests the bulk of its financial assets in overseas branches—NBAD has 14 including a wholly owned subsidiary in Washington, D.C. In Sharjah a number of investment companies have taken root, notable among them the Sharjah Group.

The revenue squeeze resulting from the oil glut of the early 1980s left some local banks overextended, notably Dubai's Union Bank of the Middle East (UBME). In November 1983 the Central Bank took over UBME to prevent its collapse and a chain of bank failures that would almost certainly have followed. This decisive and effective action has gone far to reassure those concerned with the future stability of the UAE's financial system. One possible problem, however, does lie with the courts. The Federal Supreme Court and the lower courts have taken conflicting positions on interest payments. Although regular banks continue to pay interest, an element of uncertainty remains to be resolved. Islamic banking, in which the Islamic strictures against interest on borrowed funds are observed, has been introduced to the UAE, notably with the creation of Dubai Islamic Bank, but the role Islamic banking will play in the larger financial sector has yet to be determined.

The question of whether to establish a stock exchange in the UAE has been debated for some time, and a draft law was enacted in 1983 to set one up. Although scheduled to open in 1984, it has not yet done so. Concerns over the possibility of excessive speculation by local businesses in such an exchange, fueled by the collapse of the Suq al-Manakh (unofficial stock market) in Kuwait, have helped to delay indefinitely the creation of a stock exchange in the Emirates.

FOREIGN ECONOMIC RELATIONS

As with most developing countries, the UAE's principal trade relationships are with the industrialized states. However, in the past few years several organizations have been established to promote the mutual economic welfare of the UAE and its Arab brothers (OAPEC has already been mentioned). Most significant are those focused on the Gulf, such as the OAPEC-funded Arab Company for Shipbuilding and Repair and the Arabian Gulf Organization for Industrial Consultancy. The former has tried to improve repair and maintenance capacity in the Gulf; the latter seeks to promote coordination in economic development between Gulf Arab states. Far and away the most important regional grouping of this sort is the Gulf Cooperation Council (GCC), which links the six traditional regimes of the UAE, Kuwait, Saudi Arabia, Bahrain, Qatar, and Oman.

The GCC represents a long-felt need for improved cooperation and coordination among the Gulf Arab countries on economic, security, and political matters, but it did not come into existence until 1981 when Iran and Iraq, embroiled in their war, could not effectively oppose (or join and dominate) the organization. Although concern with economic issues, pressed especially by Kuwait, was a major factor in launching the GCC, internal and external security issues have tended to dominate its deliberations and actions in the shadow of the Iran-Iraq war. Nevertheless, meaningful progress has been made on the economic front, though the goal of reaching the European Economic Community's (EEC) level of economic integration will not soon be met. Modest but useful steps have been taken.

In 1983 a "unified economic agreement" was adopted and its provision to enhance movement of goods and people implemented. Beginning March 1, 1984, citizens of any GCC state could set up business establishments in any other GCC state. Progress toward a common position on customs duties as outlined in the agreement has been harder because adoption of a common position would cause an economic loss to some emirates. Other major GCC undertakings include the development of a grid that links member gas fields with industrial consuming centers and the Gulf Investment Corporation's commitment to finance projects in accordance with a collective approach to economic issues—construction of an oil refinery in Oman is one specific involvement under consideration. Although dramatic movement toward economic unity is not a current prospect, the modest, pragmatic accomplishments in place thus far as well as contemplated future steps bode well for the GCC's survival and continued usefulness in promoting economic development. As the third wealthiest GCC member (after Saudi Arabia and Kuwait), the UAE has played an important role, at the head-of-state and ministerial levels, in the organization's economic affairs and will continue to do so.

Economic Relations with Iraq and Iran

UAE economic relations with the major Arab state in the Gulf—
Iraq—have not developed to a great extent, partly because until the
recent past Iraq has been politically hostile to the UAE and its fellow
conservative regimes. In the course of the Iran-Iraq war the UAE has
been obliged to become a financial supporter of the Baghdad government, though of the estimated $40 billion loaned or given to Iraq
by late 1984, the lion's share has come from Saudi Arabia.

Among the six GCC states the UAE has by far the most extensive
trade relations with Iran, mainly because Dubai has long had an
important economic relationship with Iran. The 1984 posting of two
trade attachés to Iran's embassy in Abu Dhabi indicates a reinforcement
of business relations between Iran and the UAE as a whole. In contrast
with the other GCC states, the UAE's mutually beneficial trade with
Iran is governed by a business-as-usual attitude.

After the imposition of western sanctions against Khomeini's
government, Dubai built up its re-export trade with Iran. Although
the Iran-Iraq war has reduced this trade, it was substantial enough
in 1983 to provide Dubai with a trade surplus despite falling oil
revenues. The Dubai tie is of great importance to Iran because not
only does Iran thereby receive vital re-export items but also remittances
from the estimated 60,000 Iranians (more than 75 percent of the total
number of Iranians in the UAE) who work in Dubai. Participation
by Iran and the UAE in each other's trade fairs and increased air
passenger and freight traffic suggest growing business ties.[11] The
continuing, indeed improving, economic links with Iran help to some
extent to insulate the UAE against the security threat from across the
Gulf and could help to pave the way to an enhanced relationship in
the postwar period.

Imports and Exports

UAE exports to all destinations dropped from a peak of $22
billion in 1980 (with slightly more than $20 billion represented by
oil and gas) to $15.4 billion in 1983 (with $12.8 generated by
hydrocarbons). Figures released by the UAE Ministry of Planning
indicate that the values of exports for 1984 remained virtually the
same as for 1983; at the same time, imports declined by almost $1.4
billion, leving a surplus of about $9 billion.[12] In 1983 Japan received
one-half of all the UAE's exports, with France a distant second at 8
percent and the United States fifth with 3.5 percent.

As with its exports, the great bulk of the UAE's import trade
is with the advanced industrial nations. In 1983 Japan was first,

supplying 19 percent of the country's imports. The United States was next with approximately 12 percent, and the United Kingdom held a similar share of the market, with West Germany and Italy in fourth and fifth positions. The leading items in the country's imports from the Western countries and Japan are heavy construction equipment (including oil field supplies), motor vehicles, engines and generators, air-conditioning systems, and the television sets, VCRs, and stereo systems that have become so much a part of the UAE environment. The United States continues to compete well in the important UAE market for medical equipment and supplies and in the current leading growth sector for imports—computers and word processors.

Although trade relations with the Eastern Bloc countries have not been important in quantitative terms—imports from communist countries were 3.5 percent by value in 1977 and have declined since— there have been noteworthy developments. East Germany, Hungary, and Rumania have established trade offices in the UAE. Bulgaria's national airline and the USSR's Aeroflot both maintain offices in the UAE and make regularly scheduled flights. Among the communist trading partners the People's Republic of China has been the most important by a wide margin, providing some $134 million in imports in 1980 out of a total of $196 million from the communist world.[13] It is possible that the 1984 establishment of diplomatic relations with the PRC will further enhance the economic relationship.

Economic Assistance to Developing Nations

Another important aspect of the UAE's international economic relations is the program of economic assistance to poor developing nations—in essence an Abu Dhabi program. The principle mechanism for delivering assistance has been the Abu Dhabi Fund for Arab Economic Development (ADFAED). Chartered in 1971 and put into operation in 1974, it was modeled largely on the Kuwait Fund for Arab Economic Development and reflected both a sense of obligation to other Arab states and a realization of the pragmatic economic and political benefits of such an undertaking. Although, as the fund's name suggests, attention has been focused on the Arab world, some forty poor African and Asian countries have benefited from its assistance. ADFAED extends most of its aid in the form of concessional (i.e., low interest) loans made for ten to twenty years or longer with, usually, an initial grace period of several years. It favors projects in which its contributions meet up to one-half the total cost. ADFAED carefully evaluates projects to be certain they merit support and then follows up with an appraisal when the project is completed.

Abu Dhabi's aid program has been very generous: In some years its grants and loans have accounted for as much as 20 percent of the emirate's gross domestic product. By the end of 1982 ADFAED had loaned more than $1 billion to developing countries, while nearly $500 million had been expended in the form of technical assistance. Beyond that, the Abu Dhabi government and Shaikh Zayed personally had given more than $600 million, which was administered by ADFAED. However, the precipitous decline in the emirate's oil revenues has forced a sharp reduction in the aid program that hit heavily in 1983, though there had been some decline each year from the 1978 peak. Nevertheless, the fund is replenished by loan payments and now manages a total of $1.7 billion in funds. Despite the fact that for some time the scope of ADFAED's loans and grants will be significantly reduced, the essential commitment to substantial assistance for carefully considered projects remains unaltered.

PROBLEMS AND PROSPECTS FOR THE UAE ECONOMY

The dominant issue for the UAE economy in the early and mid-1980s had, of course, been the worldwide oil glut and the resulting decline in the country's oil revenues. This was brought home by the deficits in both the federal and Abu Dhabi budgets in 1983—$1.49 billion and $760 million respectively. However, although deficits in an enormously wealthy country are, at least superficially, a striking phenomenon, the gravity of the situation can easily be exaggerated. The federal budgets are not entirely meaningful because the individual emirates tend to exercise great autonomy over spending plans, and the emirates have their own budgets, which do not affect the federal budget. The 1984 federal deficit was expected to be reduced by about one-fifth and Abu Dhabi's by nearly one-half through the practice of holding spending levels steady. The country's balance of payments has remained in a surplus situation, though by a smaller margin. Even though Dubai's exports and, especially, its re-exports went down substantially in 1984, its oil revenues (by contrast with Abu Dhabi's) stayed high, assuring that emirate a trade surplus not far off from its record 1983 figure. What is somewhat more worrisome is the outflow of private and institutional capital because of the lack of investment opportunities in the country.

The decline in UAE revenues has meant a general slowdown in economic activity, and Abu Dhabi, which bears both the brunt of the OPEC output reductions and the greatest responsibility for federal expenditures, has been hardest hit by the economic downturn. To some degree, however, Abu Dhabi has been insulated against the full impact of the oil revenue cutback because oil earnings are denominated in dollars and the UAE currency—the *dirham*—is linked to a strong, appreciating dollar. The deficits do signify a tightening of capital, and the principal concern of those affected is how the government chooses to deal with that situation. Partly, the government has responded to economic downturn by cutting significantly the outlay for salaries of government personnel, with some negative impact on bureaucratic morale. The major means of trimming expenditures to fit reduced revenue is a government slowdown or deferral of various projects. Several major construction schemes designed to reshape the city of Abu Dhabi in a very extensive way, including a series of bridges linking Abu Dhabi and adjacent islands, have been shelved, at least for now. Although other large remaining infrastructure projects, like the new airport at al-Ain, are proceeding, their completion dates are being moved back. (At the end of 1984, Dubai's level of construction activity appeared higher than Abu Dhabi's.) Moreover, ministry payments to contractors have slowed (though the government has denied a deliberate policy in this regard), thereby braking the outflow of government expenditures.

There has been an uncomfortable squeeze for contractors in the construction sector and nervousness in some of the banks that have extended loans to contractors. Apparently, with basic infrastructure needs close to being met and the prospect of a reduced level of economic activity, the government has decided not to finance the deficits, i.e., to forego economic pump-priming and permit some shaking out in the economy. Following the earlier years of unusually high levels of economic acvitivy, when many made easy profits, a kind of Darwinian process of natural selection will weed out many of the weaker enterprises. This is a necessary part of the maturing process in the economy. The UAE will certainly remain a rich market for stronger, better organized companies, both foreign and domestic. Moreover, the essential economic strength of the two wealthy emirates, Abu Dhabi and Dubai, remains impressive, with their basic assets greatly superior to their commitments, and the recent economic performance of the poorer northern emirates has been encouraging.

There are, in fact, reasons to see a silver lining in the clouds of economic recession. The recession has forced a serious reassessment of economic development strategy in the UAE, leading to more rational and efficient utilization of resources. As noted earlier, the recession has prompted an emphasis on enhancing the role of locally run business enterprises in providing goods and services. If managed properly, the slowdown will provide a healthy, indeed necessary, transitional adjustment to more modest rates of economic growth after the abnormal boom of the late 1970s. Moreover, the slump in the economy has produced a significant emigration of foreign workers. Although their departure adds somewhat to the slump (by reducing net consumption of goods and services), in the long run this emigration will have a positive social and political impact by reducing both the relative and absolute size of the foreign community.

The oil market will surely improve from the low point of 1983-1984, but it is equally certain that contraction of the UAE economy will lead, over time, to more slowly paced economic growth. With the completion of the nation's basic economic infrastructure in sight, greater attention will be turned to the problems of operating and maintaining what has been built. There will also be a shift of emphasis to further developing small and medium industry, the service economy, and the human resources needed to run them.

Abu Dhabi will try to husband its enormous oil and gas reserves and compete in the international market with its downstream products (i.e., refined goods derived from crude oil). Although it will press development outside the hydrocarbon sector, most economic activity in that emirate will remain tied, directly or indirectly, to Abu Dhabi's underground source of wealth. Dubai will exhaust its oil and gas reserves sooner, but has prospects of a revived re-export trade once the Iran-Iraq war ceases to overshadow the Gulf. Its likely goal is eventually to achieve financial independence by supporting itself on the interest earned from overseas investments. (By the early 1980s Kuwait earned as much revenue from its foreign investments as from its oil exports.) Abu Dhabi might also look to such a long-term solution in order to sustain its prosperity.

NOTES

1. It has been estimated that, at the turn of the century, the pearl trade produced an annual income of about £1.5 million. That included income earned by the larger fleets of Kuwait and Bahrain in addition to what the fleets of Qatar, Oman, and the Trucial States brought in.

2. *Middle East Economic Digest* 28, no. 32 (August 10, 1984):54 (hereinafter referred to as *MEED*).

3. See Nicholas B. Angell, "Legal Factors Relating to Foreign Investment in the United Arab Emirates," memorandum prepared for the law firm of Chadbourne, Parke, Whiteside, and Wolff (October 1982) and available through the Office of the Near East, U.S. Department of Commerce, p. 13.

4. See Youssef M. Ibrahim, "United Arab Emirates Reduces Oil Prices for Firms Operating Its Production Fields," *Wall Street Journal*, November 21, 1984, p. 4. Quotation in *Wall Street Journal*, January 11, 1985, p. 1.

5. *Middle East Economic Digest Special Report: UAE* (November 1984):72 (hereinafter referred to as *MEED Special Report*).

6. Ibid.

7. See Department of State airgram, "The Greening of the United Arab Emirates," U.S. Embassy in Abu Dhabi, March 23, 1982, p. 9.

8. Nicholas B. Angell, Esq., "Regulation of Business under the Developing Legal System in the United Arab Emirates," *The Laws of Saudi Arabia, the UAE, Egypt and Jordan* (Washington, D.C.: American-Arab Affairs Council, no date of publication given but issued in 1984), pp. 15, 16, 18; J. M. Barlow, Esq., "Commercial Agency Law: Current Practice," *Middle East Executive Reports* (Washington, D.C.: July 1984), p. 23 and attached excerpts from Federal Commercial Companies Law; and Frederick W. Taylor, Jr., Esq., "The Federal Commercial Companies Law," *Middle East Executive Reports* (Washington, D.C.: June 1984):9, 20–22.

9. "Foreign Firms Reject Reinvestment Proposal" *MEED Special Report*, p. 73.

10. Address by Frederick Taylor on commercial law in the UAE before the annual meeting of the Shaybani Society, October 20, 1984, in Washington, D.C.

11. Robin Allen, "Iran-UAE Links Strengthen," *MEED* (August 31, 1984):38.

12. Figures given in "Economic Trends Report for the United Arab Emirates: July 1984," Department of State airgram, U.S. Embassy in Abu Dhabi, July 28, 1984, p. 2. Figures from other sources, including those compiled by the U.S. Department of Commerce, differ somewhat. Trade figures for 1984 cited in "Increase in 1984 Trade Surplus Registered," *Khaleej Times* (Dubai) (in English), August 2, 1985, in Foreign Broadcast Information Service, *Daily Report: Middle East and Africa* 5, no. 152 (August 7, 1985):C3.

13. Department of State airgram, "CERP 0002: Relations with Communist Countries," U.S. Embassy in Abu Dhabi, January 15, 1983, table I.

5

Domestic Politics: The Course of Federation

ESTABLISHMENT AND SURVIVAL OF THE FEDERATION

Contrary to the predictions of most outside observers at the time of the UAE's birth in December 1971, the federation has survived as a going concern well into its second decade. The external and internal threats to stability do not appear presently to endanger the UAE's existence. The relevant questions concerning the federation's near-term political prospects have to do with the pace of federal development, continuing disagreement over the desirable degree of integration, remaining privileges and prerogatives of the individual emirates, and the opening up of an elitist, paternalistic system of political authority.

In the early phase of its independent existence, the federation faced aggressions and dangers from outside its borders—Iran had seized the Gulf islands of Abu Musa and the Tunbs, Saudi Arabia claimed most of Abu Dhabi's territory, and a radical Marxist-led rebellion in neighboring Oman appeared poised to menace the entire lower Gulf. Moreover, rivalries and disputes between the seven emirates, especially those about borders, seemed likely to undermine the federation's prospects for meaningful integration. By the middle of the 1970s, however, the looming dangers from without had dissipated (see Chapter 2), and despite slow and uneven progress toward full federal integration, the UAE had demonstrated its basic viability.

Several factors, internal and external, favored unity at the outset and helped overcome doubtful or antagonistic sentiment toward the idea of union. A common political culture, rooted in traditional Arab and Islamic values and a broadly shared history, linked all seven emirates. At the same time, the very slight development of political institutions, especially outside of Abu Dhabi, Sharjah, and Dubai, made it easier for the seven emirates to come together and develop new institutions at the federal level. The rulers' common experience of British protection and the British introduction, even at a late date, of political and military institutions embracing all the emirates gave the rulers some useful experience in cooperation. The radical threats, most notably from the People's Front for the Liberation of the Occupied Arab Gulf (PFLOAG), had an effect similar to that of the dangers to the emerging United States when Banjamin Franklin advised the thirteen colonies that they "must indeed all hang together, or, most assuredly [they would] all hang separately,." Moreover, the emirates' larger, potentially rapacious neighbors—Iraq, Iran, and Saudi Arabia— all tended to checkmate one another.

A last important external circumstance was that the United States, with predominant superpower influence in the Gulf area, favored union. Finally, sober reflection persuaded the seven rulers that a go-it-alone approach was not viable—Abu Dhabi lacked the personnel to run an independent state, Dubai lacked a hinterland, and the others generally lacked these as well as wealth. Once one or two emirates had been disabused of the possibility of finding other partners with whom to link up (before joining the federation Ras al-Khaimah had even proposed to the United States a special tie giving the United States military base rights on its territory), there were no real alternatives to federation.

Before examining the federal institutions that the 1971 provisional constitution (still in effect) created, it should be observed that political authority at both the emiral and federal levels is still wielded in a very traditional way. Decisions are made by hereditary rulers and a small circle of advisers, who at senior levels are themselves largely from ruling families. Neither executive nor legislative positions are filled by elected officials; indeed, there are no elections or political parties of any sort. Yet, as we shall see, this does not mean that power is exercised arbitrarily or oppressively, nor does it mean the formal institutions that have been created, ostensibly along modern lines, are simply an artificial graft onto a mainly tribal-based system. These institutions were chosen to provide a structure to which the dynamic process of traditional politics could be adapted.

THE INSTITUTIONS OF THE FEDERAL GOVERNMENT

There are three political bodies at the federal level—the Supreme Federal Council (SFC—sometimes referred to as the Supreme Council of the Union), the Council of Ministers, and the Federal National Council (FNC). The SFC comprises the rulers of the seven emirates;

the Council of Ministers includes all the heads of federal departments and is presided over by a prime minister; and the FNC is an advisory body whose members are appointed by the rulers. The UAE's president and vice president are elected by the SFC.

The SFC represents the highest political authority in the UAE. It charts the general policy of the federation, elects the president and vice president, ratifies federal laws and international treaties, and prepares the federal budget. With an annual term of eight months and ordinary sessions scheduled every two months, the SFC usually meets four times a year. Each ruler has a single vote and, although procedural issues are decided by a simple majority vote, all substantive matters require the assent of five rulers, including those of both Abu Dhabi and Dubai.

The president exercises fairly substantial authority in the UAE's political system, which is a mix of the presidential and the parliamentary. His powers are both exclusive and shared. In his own right he performs numerous ceremonial and procedural functions, such as convening the SFC and presiding over its meetings. He represents the UAE in its foreign relations, supervises the implementation of federal laws and decrees, can pardon or commute penalties imposed by the courts, and must approve any death penalty. The president appoints the prime minister with the approval of the SFC and selects the deputy prime minister(s) and ministers in consultation with the prime minister. With the approval of Council of Ministers he appoints senior government officials and diplomatic representatives. Because he is given the responsibility for calling joint meetings between the SFC and the Council of Ministers when necessary, he plays a crucial role in linking the federation's two principal political bodies. The president has been described as a balancer who, with the prime minister, serves largely to regulate conflicts within the political system.[1] Elected to a term of five years, the president may be reelected indefinitely; Shaikh Zayed, first elected in 1971, has been the UAE's only president.

The actual seat of legislative authority is the Council of Ministers, the federal cabinet, made up of the prime minister, presently two deputy prime ministers, and a number of ministers and ministers-of-state (sixteen ministers and six ministers-of-state following the reshuffle of July 8, 1983). Most laws are initiated in the council, which also establishes regulations necessary to implement federal laws. Among the council's other functions are the preparation of the federal budget and supervision of the implementation of all federal laws, decrees, and regulations, Supreme Court decisions, and international treaties and other agreements.

The Federal National Council superficially appears closest to being a parliament or legislature. Its forty members are chosen from the seven emirates according to a weighted formula reflecting the population and influence of each; thus, Abu Dhabi and Dubai are each allotted eight seats, Sharjah and Ras al-Khaimah six each, and the remaining emirates of Fujairah, Ajman, and Umm al-Qaiwain four apiece. Delegates serve two year terms, renewable without limit. The FNC meets in annual sessions of not less than six months beginning in November, though extraordinary sessions may be called at other times. Its real power is virtually nil because it does not initiate legislation but only offers recommendations on draft laws issued by the Council of Ministers, which is not, in turn, obliged to accept any of the FNC's proposals. Although the FNC may prove to be a useful exercise in developing political expertise and leadership and might someday provide the basis for a real legislature, it is now only a consultative institution and debating forum, entirely dominated by the Council of Ministers.

The judicial branch of the federal government is represented by a Supreme Court and several Courts of First Instance. The UAE president, with SFC approval, appoints a president and a maximum of five judges to the Supreme Court. Judges in all courts are considered independent of other government authority and hold indefinite terms until resignation, subject to dismissal only in extraordinary circumstances. The principal functions of the Supreme Court are adjudication of disputes between an emirate and the federal government or between individual emirates, determination of the constitutionality of federal or state laws if contested, resolution of jurisdictional disputes between federal and emirate systems or between the courts of two or more emirates, and adjudication of crimes against the state, such as those affecting its security.

The Federal Courts of First Instance deal with administrative, commercial, and civil disputes between the federal government and individuals. They also have jurisdiction over crimes and other legal infractions in the federal capital. The constitution leaves other judicial matters to local judicial bodies in the emirates, while indicating that their prerogatives could be transferred to the Courts of First Instance. This, in fact, has progressively occurred since the mid-1970s.

The system of law in the UAE is drawn from various sources, including European ones (see the discussion of business law in Chapter 4), but with a special emphasis on Islamic law (the Sharia), an emphasis that has recently increased. The constitution itself is a blend of Western and Islamic principles.[2] Since independence the court system has been staffed in large part by expatriates from several

Arab countries. Although the present training of fairly considerable numbers of UAE citizens in law will eventually alter that situation, foreign judges still play an important role in administering the law.

The UAE Civil Service

To run the government of the new state a federal civil service, based mainly in Abu Dhabi, was created in 1973. Its expansion was rapid until the oil revenue squeeze of the early 1980s prompted a cutback in its numbers. The service began with fewer than 4,000 civil employees, but within ten years the bureaucracy had swelled to more than 40,000. The rapidity of this growth has inevitably led to considerable inefficiency, and the problem of overstaffing is addressed only when prompted by the need for budgetary cuts. Thus, the 1984 federal draft budget allotted 10 percent less for government salaries than had the 1983 budget. Although some confusion and loss of morale may result, the need to trim the size of the overgrown civil service does provide an opportunity for making it more efficient.

The unavailability of trained UAE citizens in anything like the necessary numbers has made inevitable a considerable dependence on expatriates. Egyptians, Palestinians, Syrians, and others play a key role in running the various parts of the federal administration. Indeed, non-nationals continue to outnumber locals in most ministries, though key senior positions in the government are kept in the hands of citizens.

Among nationals, the largest number of civil servants has come from Dubai, reflecting the level of skills in that emirate and the lack of incentive in Abu Dhabi, given its rapid infusion of wealth and elaborate social welfare system, for its inhabitants to seek public employment. A major problem in recruiting capable public servants has been that most bright and energetic young Emirians, at least in the wealthier emirates, are drawn into business where pecuniary rewards have been much greater. Nevertheless, in spite of excessive growth, reliance on outsiders, and failure to attract the best and brightest native talents, the UAE bureaucracy has effectively carried out the task of dispensing vital economic and social services to the nation's population as well as providing the support infrastructure for the population's ongoing development. The federal administration has taken the government into every part of the UAE, thus playing a crucial role in making a reality of the federal union.

One problem for the federal administration as it has developed is the fundamental ambivalence and confusion between federal and emirate-level authority. Initially, many public service functions remained in the domain of the individual emirate governments. But once Abu Dhabi terminated its emiral cabinet in late 1973, other emirates generally followed suit, though some overlap continues and adds to the inefficiency of the bureaucracy. The constitution leaves somewhat fuzzy the delineation of powers delegated to the federal government and those reserved to the member emirates. That reflects the reality of divisions between individual rulers about how much authority the federal government should have and presents one of the main challenges to the nation's political leadership.

POLITICAL LEADERSHIP AND CHALLENGES

Beneath the formal institutions described above, the political life of the country continues to be conducted in a largely traditional way. Political leadership is essentially hereditary and ascriptive, rather than elective and meritocratic. The essence and symbol of the traditional system is the *majlis*, the formal consultation mechanism that brings ruler and subjects (male only) together, enabling the latter to raise grievances, present petitions, and generally discuss issues of concern to them. Relying on this long established system, which gives the people close access to their ruler and puts him in close touch with their needs and sentiments, the tribal shaikh has dispensed justice, exercised control of his subjects, and maintained his legitimacy. If it is far removed from Western political democracy, it nevertheless represents a highly effective form of social democracy that has retained its essential vitality and viability to the present time. Thus, although twenty-five years ago the conventional wisdom held that such systems were curious anachronisms ready to collapse of their own weight, yielding to Nasserism and other brave new Arab ideologies, these systems have survived, while it is the latter that are endangered species. At the same time, given the endurance of the traditional system of rule, relatively little political awareness has developed among the people.

Political power in each emirate rests with the ruling families and is exercised through the *diwan*, the traditional institution in which advisers appointed by the amiral ruler represent important segments of the society and assist the ruler. In each case the rulers' families are part of the most powerful tribal grouping, and, except in the case of Ras al-Khaimah, their tribes are also the largest. Shaikh Zayed of Abu Dhabi is a member of the Al Nuhayyan, a family that in turn is part of the Al Bu Falah, the small but predominant subtribe within the Bani Yas, the largest tribe—more accurately, tribal con-federation—in the UAE. Shaikh Rashid of Dubai is of the Maktum family, part of a rival subtribe, the Al Bu Falasah, within the Bani Yas, which broke away a century and a half ago to settle in Dubai. The rulers of Sharjah and Ras al-Khaimah are of different families from within the Qasimi tribe that at one time (see the historical background in Chapter 2) dominated the area. In the same fashion, the rulers of Ajman, Umm al-Qaiwain, and Fujairah are paramount chiefs of, respectively, the Nu'aimi, Mu'alla, and Sharqi tribes.

Leadership Among the Al Nuhayyan

Because Shaikh Zayed's position as leader of the UAE derives from his exercise of authority as ruler of Abu Dhabi, it is pertinent to explore the bases of that authority. Zayed's family, the Al Nuhayyan, has ruled Abu Dhabi for about two centuries, and he is the brother, son, and grandson of rulers. However, although rulership has remained within one family, the absence of a regular rule of succession in Arab tribal politics can generate potential divisions within the family. (It is only in the last few years that the eldest son has generally been designated to succeed his father.) Zayed and his elder brother Shakhbut, whom he succeeded, are of the Sultan branch of the Al Nuhayyan; their predecessors were of the Khalifa branch. Although at this point little danger of an active challenge from the Khalifa exists, Zayed has been careful to accord its members an appropriate share of power in an astute balancing act within the family. Thus, Shaikh Mubarak bin Muhammad Al Nuhayyan of the rival branch is federal minister of the interior, and one of his brothers, Shaikh Suroor bin Muhammad Al Nuhayyan, is a key adviser to Zayed.

Outside the ruling family, the other significant elements in the elite emiral system of political power are the religious establishment and leading commoners, often merchants, who are from families whose prominence derives from other circumstances. Thus, Shaikh Zayed and his fellow rulers have been solicitous of their relations with the *ulema*, the religious scholars who teach the principles of Islam and oversee the application of Islamic law, the Sharia. The importance of two leading families in Abu Dhabi, the Suwaidis and Otaibas, is reflected in the fact that they have been represented in the federal government by Ahmad al-Suwaidi, the first foreign minister of the UAE, now adviser to Shaikh Zayed, and Mana Said al-Otaiba, the only petroleum minister the UAE has had.

Finally, the ruler's own character and abilities are of central importance. Shaikh Zayed's leadership abilities (as evidenced in Chapter 2) have fitted him unusually well for the responsibilities he has borne as ruler of Abu Dhabi and president of the UAE. Not only does he possess abundantly the courage, shrewdness, and forebearance admired among the bedouins, whose values still shape the culture, but he has acquired a wide and penetrating awareness of the outside world with which he must deal. It was Zayed's capacity to understand and deal with the new world ushered in by oil wealth that was responsible for his displacing his older brother Shakhbut (r. 1928–1966). Lacking that capacity, Shakhbut came to be seen in both local and British eyes as too great a liability, and his peaceful removal was accordingly engineered. To earn and retain his position, a traditional ruler thus requires more than inherited position, wealth, and other advantages. Generally speaking, like Shaikh Zayed, the other emirate rulers have been perceived as embodying the important values of their society and polity and as being fair and capable; as a result, they have generally enjoyed legitimacy and popularity.

Leadership Among the Maktum

Shaikh Rashid bin Maktum is, in his own way, almost as impressive a figure as Shaikh Zayed. His skill in promoting Dubai's fortunes helped his emirate gain parity within the UAE with the much wealthier and more powerful Abu Dhabi at the time of independence. Ruler of Dubai for more than twenty-five years, Rashid has often been described as a merchant prince, a latter-day version of a Renaissance Venetian doge. His relationship to the government of Dubai has been compared to a situation in which one man is board, chairman, and chief executive of a large holding company.[3] Dubai's leading businessman as well as its ruler, he is disdainful of bureaucracy and has always sought to keep Dubai's administration lean and simple and under his watchful control.

Essentially a commercial city-state, Dubai is less tribal and more cosmopolitan than Abu Dhabi. In fact the majority of its merchants are of non-Arab origin, coming largely from Iran or the Indian subcontinent, though most have been long residents and are well settled in Dubai. The prominent men of commerce play an important role in making political and economic decisions in the emirate, characteristically guided to a very great extent by their solicitude for the state's trade links with the outside world. In addition, some Arab expatriates have played a prominent role in Dubai's politics, the best known and most powerful among them being Mahdi Tajer, a Bahraini, who directed Dubai's Office of Petroleum Affairs and has long served as UAE Ambassador in London.

As with the Al Nuhayyan in Abu Dhabi, there is a history of factionalism within the ruling Maktum clan in Dubai. However, this seems safely consigned to the past for now, and the much simpler tribal structure of the emirate's population means that there is far less concern for tribal politics than in Abu Dhabi. The prosperity enjoyed under Shaikh Rashid's patriarchal rule has made him popular and secure, and his political shrewdness has won him admiration.

Leadership in the Other Emirates

The emirate of Sharjah not only faces most of the political and administrative challenges of Abu Dhabi but must also contend with its severely segmented territory—it is the only emirate to border all the others and Oman and the only one with coastlines on both the Gulf and the Gulf of Oman. Memories of ancestral Qasimi preeminence and of Sharjah's favored place as seat of British political and military authority in the area has led to a certain resentment regarding the back seat Sharjah has taken, of necessity, to its two recently more powerful neighbors. Sharjah's municipal government, introduced some sixty years ago, has led to a well-developed emiral administration, a source of considerable pride. Sharjans are also proud of the emirate's high level of intellectual and cultural life, in part the product of its early experience of a modern school system. In this connection it is fitting that the current ruler, Shaikh Sultan bin Muhammad Al Qasimi, was the first ruler in the UAE to have a university education.

Sharjah is the emirate that most recently experienced a change of leadership through violence. In 1972 the previous ruler, Shaikh Khalid bin Muhammad, was assassinated in an attempted coup by the cousin who had earlier been removed by the British. After the assassination the new federal government intervened to prevent the coup from succeeding and, through the Supreme Federal Council, selected the slain ruler's successor. This usurpation of traditional Qasimi authority signified the weakening of the tribes' political power and the growing ascendancy of federal power in the new federation. Sultan has been secure in his rulership since his succession, and the absence of any other violent challenge to an emiral ruler, while three peaceful successions have occurred, suggests the once endemic political violence of the system has been overcome.

The rulers of Ras al-Khaimah, who are from the other branch of the Qawasim, tend to exhibit a similar resentment about the reversal of the old power relationships in the area and the emirate's consequently reduced role in the federation. Whether its independent, strong-minded ruler, Shaikh Saqr, will be more reconciled with the discovery of commercially exploitable oil—after years of fruitless search—remains to be seen. Despite a rather delicate balancing act with other tribes larger than the Qawasim, the ruler seems secure.

Umm al-Qaiwain and Ajman, where peaceful successions have recently occurred after the two longest-ruling emirs passed away, are ruled in the same way as their neighbors, as is Fujairah. The principal contrast reflects their smaller, poorer condition, which has dictated much smaller and simpler governments and administrations.

Relations Among the Seven Emirates

Some of the factors coloring relations between the seven emirates have already been suggested. Dynastic rivalries and disputes, most often involving borders and resource ownership, have at times erupted into violence. In 1972 Fujairah and Sharjah came to blows over the sovereignty of a tiny parcel of land with a well that had traditionally been used by the tribesmen of both emirates, and some twenty lives were lost before federal government intervention ended the conflict. However, although irridentist claims and other contentious issues continue to irritate interemirate relationships, many of the most dangerous conflicts have been settled, and those remaining do not appear likely to lead to open conflict. Alignments and estrangements among the emirates do, however, play a role in UAE affairs.

A "leapfrog pattern of good and bad relations" among lower Gulf rulers, extending north to Bahrain, has been noted by one observer of Gulf politics.[4] Within the UAE this traditional schema has led to the development of two groups of loosely aligned emirates— the Abu Dhabi group, which brings the rulers of Sharjah, Umm al-Qaiwain, and Fujairah into association with Shaikh Zayed, and the Dubai group, which draws the rulers of Ajman and Ras al-Khaimah into close relations with Shaikh Rashid. This is a somewhat useful key to understanding political relationships within the UAE, but the frequent splits within each group—as with the Sharjah-Fujairah dispute noted above—suggest its limitations. Moreover, as we shall see, at critical junctures Zayed and Rashid have been able to submerge their long rivalry.

That the UAE has grown and prospered as a federation in the face of jealousies, antipathies, and contentions among its constituent parts is due primarily to Shaikh Zayed's commitment to the concept of federal union and his generous dispensing of Abu Dhabi's financial support to make it a reality. The size, strength, and wealth of Abu Dhabi, with more than 85 percent of the federation's territory, 40 percent of its population, the greatest portion of its military forces, and funds that supply more than 90 percent of the federal budget and have for an extended period of time, has made it the "overwhelming core" of the federation.[5] This control of the bulk of the federation's resources has been crucial in sustaining Abu Dhabi's efforts to promote union. Moreover, Shaikh Zayed has been prepared to make very considerable political sacrifices for the UAE's success, as was evident in his willingness to accord parity to Dubai within the federation. He has made every effort to promote an equitable sharing of federal responsibilities and prerogatives among representatives of emiral, tribal, and other claims. In spite of this, the process of advancing the federation has been uneven and slow, with crises that have reflected differing perceptions by Zayed's fellow emirs of what the federation should be and his frustration at their seemingly self-serving obstructionism.

The Abu Dhabi–Dubai Rivalry

Although it was a joint, preindependence initiative by Shaikh Zayed and Shaikh Rashid that launched the initial move toward the federation that became the UAE, these two traditional rivals were subsequently at odds over the nature and pace of federal integration. Zayed, after independence, pressed for a strong federal government and an accelerated move toward its realization. By contrast, Rashid preferred a much looser arrangement in which each emirate would exercise considerable autonomy, if not independence, in many areas. In large measure this reflects the disparity in the nature and scope of their wealth. Abu Dhabi's wealth is almost entirely from oil and, since independence, has been much greater, in large part sustaining the concrete accomplishments of the federation. Dubai, despite its considerable oil revenues, continues to depend for much of its income on trade, the traditional source of its prosperity. Thus, Dubai has been much more concerned than Abu Dhabi with maintaining a laissez-faire ethos in which it can steer its economic course unimpeded by external meddling. Indeed, as we have seen, Dubai (together with the other smaller oil-producing emirates) has continued to pursue its oil production and sale unhampered by any federal regulation. Further, although Dubai benefits from the presence of several federal departments, Shaikh Rashid has resented contributing from Dubai's purse to sustain what he sees as the bloated, inefficient federal bureaucracy in Abu Dhabi, where bureaucrats' living expenses are much higher. On Abu Dhabi's part there has been some resentment that Dubai has not pulled its weight financially in the federation, having contributed much less than the 50 percent of its pledged revenues to support the federal budget and leaving Abu Dhabi to pay the great bulk of it. In addition to these differences of viewpoint, a continuing border dispute between Abu Dhabi and Dubai and, simply, their long-standing habit of rivalry stood in the way of cooperation between the two leading emirates.

The failure of Rashid and the other emirs in 1976 to ratify the draft of a permanent constitution, which would have significantly strengthened the federal government (and committed Dubai to increase its contribution to the federal budget), led to Shaikh Zayed's threat not to accept another term as UAE president. This precipitated the federation's first major political crisis and led to some concessions to the cause of a stronger federal government to induce Zayed to remain at the helm. But, in fact, little progress was made in that direction. The major concession to Zayed and those favoring an enlarged central government role was the unification of security and defense forces. However, even that concession was significantly qualified, as the regional commands into which the federal armed forces were divided retained much of the character of separate emiral forces from Abu Dhabi, Dubai, and Ras al-Khaimah. Other major issues, such as oil production (as already noted) and immigration policies, were left to the determination of the individual emirates.

The 1976 crisis was, in effect, not really resolved but overcome with temporizing measures. The major issues, including a permanent constitution, were left unsettled and precipitated another major crisis in 1979. Internal pressures within the federation were reinforced by external events in the three intervening years. Egyptian President Sadat's dramatic trip to Jerusalem and the Camp David meetings and Egyptian-Israeli peace process that followed divided the Arab world and created special discomfort for moderate Arab states like the UAE. The overthrow of the Shah in Iran and the events that followed created a sense of peril from across the Gulf. Finally, the Soviet invasion of Afghanistan and U.S. reactions to it sparked fears of superpower conflicts in the Gulf area. All of these outside dangers served to underscore the need for greater strength and unity within the UAE.

A joint session of the Federal National Council and the Council of Ministers in February 1979 produced a memorandum to the Supreme Federal Council urging adoption of several major plans to make the UAE a stronger and more cohesive federation. This precipitated a political/constitutional crisis that unfolded during the spring of 1979, with expressions of public support, including student demonstrations, for Shaikh Zayed as the supporter of speedier unification. The main issue, as a leading scholar on the UAE has put it, was "the need to make the federation more governable and its institutions more professional."[6] Shaikh Rashid continued to support a gradualist approach toward unity with considerable continuing autonomy for the individual emirates, and the crisis was resolved only with the intervention of a senior member of the ruling family of Kuwait. Rashid agreed to become prime minister, thereby bringing Dubai much closer to the side of the federalists, and a cabinet was appointed that represented a compromise between unionists and autonomists. As the extension once again of the provisional constitution in 1981 suggests, major issues remain to be resolved as the federation edges closer to developing a strong central authority.

Evolution of the Federation

The severe reduction of revenues as a result of the worldwide oil glut has made the issue of an effective federal government all the more critical. In the days of plenty the generosity of Shaikh Zayed sufficed to carry the economic and social benefits through the federal system to all parts of the country. With reduced financial resources the inadequacies of the federal machinery are more painfully apparent, and the smaller, poorer emirates are hurting. Recent federal budgets were delayed until the middle of the year by squabbles about the amount to be contributed by those emirates supporting the federal budget. Although Umm al-Qaiwain and Fujairah, with their traditionally good relations with Abu Dhabi, complain less thann Ajman, with its characteristically strained relations, all are concerned about developing a fair and effective system for sharing reduced federal funds. Indeed, Shaikh Khalid of Ras al-Khaimah, son of the ruler Shaikh Saqr who once balked at joining the federation, has urged greater action by the Supreme Federal Council in this and other areas of concern as the only federal body capable of doing so.[7] It is likely that the long-standing debate about who should own and control the UAE's resources will be engaged more forcefully. Despite Abu Dhabi's largesse, there is inevitable resentment at that emirate's ability to make decisions by virtue of its wealth; there is a widely shared feeling among the other emirates that all should have a say in determining the division of the UAE's resources as part of a common patrimony.

Thus, differing attitudes toward the federation continue to affect its evolution. Despite a shared commitment to federation, the constituent emirates and their rulers are still prone to pursuing selfish courses of action at odds with the best interests of the federation. Differing degrees of dedication to the achievement of a full federal union continue to impede its realization.

PROSPECTS FOR POLITICAL STABILITY

After a decade and a half of independence, what are the UAE's prospects for continued political survival and stability? The seven emirates and their rulers are more committed to the success of the federation than when the experiment began. The degree of mutual suspicion and distrust has diminished considerably, and the perceived benefits of federal union much outweigh the fears, now slighter than at the outset, of federal interests impinging on vital member states' interests. Finally, the simple fact that the UAE has been a going enterprise for an extended period of time has conditioned its leaders and citizens to think in terms of its continued existence.

With the situation of the UAE today far brighter than at its inception and much more positive than most people would have predicted, its prospects for the short term are certainly favorable. For the longer term, however, uncertainties loom depending on the way future challenges are faced.

Although the issue of immigration and the conditions and rights of expatriate workers has become somewhat less urgent, with a reduction in the non-national poulation, it remains a major unresolved question. The large foreign majority could undermine the sociocultural values of the country and imperil its political identity and strength. The question of whether expatriates who have rendered important services to the UAE through their labors should be offered the privileges of citizenship remains a difficult and unresolved matter with obvious and compelling arguments on both sides.

The difficulty of overcoming the assertion of individual emirates' prerogatives and preferences—one of the obstacles to regulating immigration in a more orderly way—will pose a major uncertainty for the country's future. Committed though they may be to the idea of federation, individual emirates are still inclined to pursue compelling self-interest even when this may conflict with important national interest. In the mid-1980s such a case is Dubai's and Sharjah's pursuit of friendly relations with Iran, the product of traditional ties across the Gulf and a lucrative trade for those two emirates. This puts them out in front of the federal government in its relations with the Khomeini government and subjects the central government, which has the sole authority for conducting foreign political and diplomatic relations, to embarrassment and pressure from Saudi Arabia and other neighbors. Although progress has been made toward federal integration in legal and, to some extent, economic matters, there is still a long way to go in critical areas like security, defense, and oil policy. This will continue to cloud the country's prospects for developing a strong and stable national government.

Another problem area important to the federation's prospects in the longer term is the opening up of the political system. The traditional, paternalistic systems of government, allowing easy access to the ruler, have until now served well. It is clear, however, that the complexities of governance in the contemporary world and the influence of various ideologies external to the UAE will require significant changes. Although there are no compelling demands for democracy at this point, demonstrations by students in 1979 calling for more rapid movement toward completion of the process of federal integration suggested that forces for popular involvement in the political process have been building. But if the old *majlis* system is outmoded as an institution for the effective articulation of the public interest and demands, no effective new mechanism has been created to take its place. This new mechanism might be accomplished by enlarging the powers of the Federal National Council and electing members popularly. Movement toward a more open political system may be easier as younger, less tradition-bound rulers come to power in the various emirates.

As the political system is made more open it will face increasingly the problem of containing ideological forces. In the past, leftist doctrines, whether advanced by revolutionary South Yemen and Omani rebels or Ba'thist governments in Iraq, were most feared. Now the Islamic resurgence, most dramatically and menacingly represented in the Iranian revolution, is a more compelling present danger. Real as these threats may be, the inherently conservative nature of the UAE society and its essential moderation and pragmatism are likely to remain proof against contending ideological forces for now. The longer term remains much less certain as the traditional, paternalistic system of political authority evolves toward some new form of government whose nature cannot yet be more than dimly envisioned.

Finally, in a nation where hereditary rule still prevails, the question of succession looms large. As noted earlier in this chapter, in a break with tradition, the eldest son has been designated as heir-apparent, thus giving the process an orderly, nonviolent character it previously lacked. What is especially of concern now is the impact of succession in Dubai and Abu Dhabi when Shaikh Rashid and Shaikh Zayed, the two dominant figures in the federation, pass from the scene. Since 1981 Shaikh Rashid has been incapacitated by serious illness and unable actively to govern Dubai and serve as UAE prime minister. His eldest son Maktum has begun, as designated heir, to assume some of his father's duties, but the situation is somewhat muddled and uncertain as long as Rashid survives and Maktum is unable to rule in his own right. He is capable and a committed federalist. At the same time it may be hard, in the midst of change and complexity, to maintain the kind of popularity and loyalty that Shaikh Rashid has for so long enjoyed.

Succeeding Shaikh Zayed will be an even greater challenge for his son Khalifa. The heir-apparent has for some years been given an increasing number of responsibilities to perform in his father's stead, as preparation for his eventual assumption of power. Despite his evident ability, Khalifa displays an obvious reluctance for the role he is destined to play. It cannot be expected that he will necessarily have his father's flair and natural gifts for rulership. This makes all the more urgent the substantive institutionalization of political authority before Shaikh Zayed, still hale and hearty but nearing the age of seventy, ceases to guide the fortunes of Abu Dhabi and the UAE.

The terms of the UAE's president and vice president expire this year. When a decision is made on the provisional constitution, the UAE's prospects may become somewhat clearer. It is doubtful that hard decisions—especially those touching on the division of powers between the central government and the emirates—can again be deferred as they were in 1976 and 1981. How those decisions are made will, in large measure, determine the UAE's prospects for continued survival and stability.

NOTES

1. Enver M. Khoury, *The United Arab Emirates: Its Political System and Politics* (Hyattsville, Md.: Institute of Middle Eastern and North African Affairs, 1980), p. 87.

2. Ali Mohammed Khalifa, *The United Arab Emirates: Unity in Fragmentation* (Boulder, Colo.: Westview Press, 1979), p. 37.

3. John Duke Anthony, *Arab States of the Lower Gulf: People, Politics, Petroleum* (Washington, D.C.: The Middle East Institute, 1975), p. 154.

4. Ibid., p. 109.

5. Khalifa, *Unity in Fragmentation*, p. 125.

6. Frauke Heard-Bey, *From Trucial States to United Arab Emirates* (London and New York: Longman, 1982), p. 399.

7. "Learning to Live Without Federal Funds," *The Middle East*, no. 125 (March 1985):21.

6

The Regional and International Arenas: Security Dangers and Prospects

On the eve of independence, the UAE's security was far from assured: The Shah's Iran seized three Gulf islands that belonged to Sharjah and Ras al-Khaimah; in Oman's Dhofar province a leftist guerrilla movement sought to overthrow the Sultan and subsequently the other conservative Gulf states; and the UAE's largest neighbor, Saudi Arabia, laid claim to much of Abu Dhabi and refused to establish diplomatic relations with the UAE. Although the Khomeini government still holds the islands, the Dhofar rebel movement has ceased to exist, Saudi Arabia has long since settled its claim and become a close ally, and other early threats have faded or been accommodated. Other dangers have emerged to pose a new challenge, but the UAE has demonstrated its ability to survive external threats.

After the establishment of the federation the UAE quickly developed its diplomatic relations with nations throughout the noncommunist world. It has important, far-flung ties in the political, economic, and security spheres. As one would expect, its closest relations tend to be within the Arab world. The UAE's primary relationships are with the other five Arab states bordering the Gulf—Saudi Arabia, Kuwait, Bahrain, Qatar, and Oman. These six nations share conservative, hereditary regimes and traditional, strongly Islamic societies as well as closely related, vital economic and security interests. The latter are reflected in their formal grouping as members of the Gulf Cooperation Council, to be discussed in this chapter.

Generally speaking, the UAE's relations are warm and close with these neighbors. The "leapfrog" pattern of relations noted earlier within the UAE does extend externally: Abu Dhabi has had traditionally good relations with Bahrain, while Abu Dhabi's rival, Dubai, has

136

maintained especially friendly ties with Qatar, Bahrain's long-standing rival. However, if these historic bonds and rivalries still color relationships, they do not determine them. Moreover, since unification and independence, the UAE's neighbors have declined to pursue special relations with individual emirates, even when approached to do so, seeing their interests best served by a viable, independent federation.

It will be recalled from Chapter 3 that both Oman and Saudi Arabia challenged the UAE at independence as to the borders it had inherited from the era of British protection. Disagreements about the common border of Oman and several emirates remain, but they are more in the nature of irritants in a generally friendly relationship than potential causes of real crisis. The Saudi conflict with Abu Dhabi about their common border, involving the greater part of the emirate's territory and considerable oil reserves as well as touching on Saudi *amour propre* after the bitter Buraini dispute with the British, was more worrisome. For nearly three years the Saudis withheld diplomatic recognition of the new nation until, finally, the matter was resolved. Since then Saudi Arabia has been generally supportive of the UAE and has been a prime source of external encouragement in favor of its unity.

Relations are generally close with the other conservative Gulf Arab countries. Bahrain and Qatar share many features and face common dangers with the UAE; past rivalries have been largely set aside in the interest of friendly cooperation. Kuwait, with a legacy of gratefully remembered assistance to the emirates in the years before wealth and independence, has a particularly close relationship with the UAE. (Its physical distance from the UAE has ensured the absence of the kinds of quarrels common to closer neighbors.) More distant—physically, politically, and culturally—from the UAE are the remaining Arabian Peninsula states of the Yemen Arab Republic (North Yemen) and the People's Democratic Republic of Yemen (PDRY—South Yemen). By contrast with the states on the Gulf side of the Arabian Peninsula, the Yemens, particularly South Yemen, are politically radical (though beneath the surface their societies are still largely traditional) and extremely poor. (The latter condition may be ameliorated if recent commercially viable oil discoveries in each country are sufficiently extensive.) Although the UAE is wary of the PDRY's Marxist radicalism and keenly remembers the Aden government's support of the PFLOAG, it has improved its relations with that country. In conjunction with Kuwait and Saudi Arabia, the UAE has sought to induce South Yemen to pursue a more moderate course by holding out the prospect of badly needed economic aid as a quid pro quo. These efforts appear to have enjoyed some success with South Yemen's leader, Ali Nasir Muhammad, who has endeavored to move the PDRY toward a less confrontational stance with its neighbors. In 1983 patient diplomacy by the UAE and Kuwait bore fruit in bringing about a rapprochement between South Yemen and Oman. South Yemen ceased to support the remnants of the radical PFLOAG movement. The two countries have established diplomatic relations for the first time and, with continuing reliance on the good offices of Kuwait and the UAE, have pursued ongoing negotiations aimed at settling their disputed common border. UAE relations with the less radical North Yemen, also a recipient of UAE aid, are good. Shaikh Zayed, who traces his distant ancestry to this part of the Arabian Peninsula, is funding construction of a new Marib dam, replacing the fabled ancient dam—destroyed some fifteen hundred years ago—and promoting agricultural development in that part of Yemen.

THE GULF COOPERATION COUNCIL AND THE UAE

However, the UAE enjoys its closest relations with the five Gulf Arab states with whom it shares membership in the GCC. In a modest, measured way the GCC has made useful progress in promoting the shared economic and security concerns of its members.

Efforts to promote cooperation and unity among the countries of the Gulf antedate the GCC. In 1975 the Shah of Iran put forward a proposal for a Gulf states security pact. The Saudis and smaller Gulf states did not then see sufficient threat to warrant such a pact and feared Iranian hegemonic ambitions. Thus, the Iran initiative came to nothing. With the fall of the Shah in 1979, despite his long-standing military security relationship with the United States, and the Soviet invasion of Afghanistan later that same year, the Gulf Arab states intensified their consultations on possible joint security measures. The outbreak of the Iran-Iraq war in September 1980 provided the final impetus for a new initiative and the possibility of undertaking it without interference from powerful neighbors. Conflict between these two dominant Gulf powers raised the specter of overt military or subversive actions by either combatant against the Gulf Arab states. It also raised the possibility that outside powers might intervene to preserve access to the Gulf's oil, adding to the fear of Soviet-U.S. rivalry intruding into the Gulf in the wake of the Soviet invasion of Afghanistan and the establishment by President Jimmy Carter of a U.S. Rapid Deployment Force to counter any further Soviet military move.

Thus, the UAE joined with its neighbors (at Saudi initiative) to consider increased cooperation among the six conservative Gulf Arab states. A series of meetings in early 1981 gave rise to the Gulf Cooperation Council. Although concern with the security threat prompted creation of the GCC, its economic role was emphasized at the outset and has remained important. A constitution was carefully drafted to define the criteria for membership so as to exclude any other states and preserve the cohesion of the organization. Iraq (which as a member would dominate the group and presumably direct Iranian hostility toward it) and North Yemen, which had expressed interest in joining, were the countries at whom this exclusion was aimed.[1] On May 25, 1981, the first GCC summit meeting, bringing together the six heads of state, was held in Abu Dhabi. In the fall the council was formally inaugurated in Saudi Arabia, at meetings in Taif and Riyadh, the latter city having been selected as the seat of the GCC Secretariat. Abdullah Bishara, an experienced Kuwaiti diplomat, was chosen secretary-general.

The Supreme Council, consisting of the six heads of state, sets policy for the GCC and is mandated by the charter to convene once every six months. The Ministerial Council, comprising the six foreign ministers, is required to meet bimonthly and report to the Supreme Council. More frequent meetings of these bodies are held when necessitated by urgent events, and there are numerous gatherings of other ministers, including those in charge of information and internal security. Increased and regular communication and consultation among the six member states on a range of issues is one of the GCC's key achievements.

Though GCC members are closely bound by shared values and interests, there are frictions and differences among them. Kuwait is at the "left" end of the GCC spectrum, striking a neutral position between the two superpowers and within the Arab world, while Oman is on the "right," granting base access and equipment prepositioning rights to the United States and defying most of the rest of the Arab world in maintaining diplomatic ties with Egypt after Camp David. Among the other members the UAE is generally closest to Kuwait, sharing in degree its opposition to the closeness of Oman to the United States. Both the UAE and Kuwait consider a superpower rivalry more likely to endanger the Gulf as a result. However, in a move that caught most observers by surprise, Oman established diplomatic relations with the Soviet Union in September 1985, and the UAE did so in November of the same year.

The more conservative members of the GCC (Saudi Arabia, Oman, Qatar, and Bahrain) have also been concerned about the radical political influence of Palestinians and other Arabs in the UAE, and Saudi Arabia, in particular, has been upset about the close ties of Dubai and Sharjah with Iran. Further, as observed in Chapter 4, the UAE has engaged in a bit of foot-dragging on progress toward a GCC customs union.

GCC Defense

However, in regard to economic and security issues the degree of cooperation among the six states has been impressive, and the UAE has contributed actively to the progress that has been made. As noted earlier, pragmatic, measured steps have been taken toward the ambitious goals (i.e., an EEC-style union) set for economic integration. The creation of an effective GCC security structure capable of defense against most enemies has proved more difficult.

An attempted coup against the government of Bahrain in December 1981, involving dissident Shias from that country and several other GCC countries supported and trained by Iran, prompted heightened anxiety about internal subversion. The coup was thwarted when some of the subversives were discovered in the UAE en route to Manama, permitting a timely warning to Bahraini authorities. Frightened by a threat that had come close to materializing and realizing the need to enhance cooperation on internal security matters, the GCC countries set about creating a formal mechanism to deal with such problems. In February 1982 the UAE, following Bahrain, signed a security cooperation agreement with Saudi Arabia, which called for regular meetings between border security officials, regular exchanges of information, and new procedures for extradition of criminals. In the same month the first meeting of the GCC's interior ministers was held to promote communication and cooperation in matters of security. Other meetings have followed. It was anticipated that the several bilateral agreements made outside the GCC would be superseded by a multilateral pact embracing all the GCC members. However, as of spring 1985, Kuwait had yet to agree to an internal security accord, apparently for fear of compromising its more liberal extradition policy. Nevertheless, the agreements among the other five have significantly upgraded their capacity to deal with subversive threats.

However, progress in developing a meaningful capacity in the GCC states for external defense against possible regional threats— which range from border incursions by the Yemenis to overland invasions (by Iraq, and possibly Iran), air-naval assault (by Iraq and Iran) to air strikes (by Iraq, Iran, or Israel)—has been slighter. The military weakness of individual Gulf states reflects the recent date at which development of sizable, modern forces was inaugurated in the GCC countries. (Saudi Arabia has a much longer history of military development, but the process has been an uneven one, owing to the government's ambivalence about a powerful, modernized military structure.)

In the UAE failure to achieve greater military strength also has been a product of the continued political divisions described in Chapter 5 and, as with the other GCC states, results also from a lack of skilled manpower. The bulk of the army's manpower and cadre of noncommissioned officers is provided by Omanis and Baluchis and, although able UAE officers have entered military service, there is continued reliance on Jordanians, Pakistanis, and Britons in senior and technical staff positions.[2] Similarly, in the vital area of air defense, the GCC countries have had to depend on expatriate expertise to a considerable extent. The UAE has developed a nucleus of skilled pilots, but its air force draws heavily on Pakistanis, Jordanians, and Moroccans.[3] Despite vast sums spent on modern weapons systems—each GCC member spends about one-third of its budget on defense, with Saudi Arabia having the highest per capita level of expenditure in the world, followed closely by the UAE—the UAE and its neighbors remain highly vulnerable to external threats. Because air defense is the most critical area of concern, given the importance and vulnerability of GCC states' oil, desalination, and other facilities, an agreement was reached in 1982 to create a common air defense system.

The air defense was to be based on the Air Warning and Command System (AWACS) that the United States had then just agreed to sell to Saudi Arabia. However, political differences among the six countries make standardization of aircraft unattainable: The UAE, Kuwait, and Qatar were turning for their purchases mainly to France; Saudi Arabia and Bahrain (acquiring aircraft for the first time) were buying aircraft from the United States; and Oman was pledged to rely on British aircraft. Lack of interoperability among these various air defense systems compromises the crucial acquisition, exchange, and utilization of "real time intelligence"—the command, control, communications, and intelligence (C^3I) aspect of those systems. Even with UAE acquisition of an advanced British C^3I and air control and warning (AC&W) system, the capacity for linkage with the Saudi system will be less than ideal.[4]

Nevertheless, the GCC states have demonstrated their determination to create a credible Gulf air defense. The Saudi downing of one or two (accounts differ) Iranian F-4s in June 1984, following an intrusion into Saudi-claimed air space, was more a demonstration of psychological will than technological capacity. Although the Saudis and other Gulf Arabs were very low key about their successful demonstration of air defense capabilities, it doubtless provided a fillip to all of them. In late 1984 a series of aerial exercises was initiated among the GCC states; the UAE engaged in exercises with both Kuwait (October) and Saudi Arabia (November). (Exercises were planned for 1985 involving all the GCC air forces but were not carried out.) Despite inherent obstacles, this suggests that the GCC is moving collectively toward a more credible air defense capability. The GCC states, with some degree of cooperation, may be able to cope with a severely attrited Iranian air force but could not, in the near future, face with any real hope of successful defense an attack from the other major regional powers, let alone a great power from outside the Middle East.

Although GCC efforts have been focused on creating an effective air defense, the decision to do so was made within the wider context of resolutions adopted at a GCC defense ministers meeting to create a GCC arms industry, coordinate military purchases among GCC members, and set up a joint rapid deployment force. These resolutions were ratified by the six rulers in November 1982. The most visible progress has since been made in setting up the GCC's rapid deployment force. In October 1983 its first exercise, code-named Peninsula Shield, was held in the western desert region of Abu Dhabi. Shaikh Khalifa bin Zayed, Abu Dhabi heir-apparent and deputy supreme commander of the UAE's armed forces, declared on that occasion that the GCC states were "fully committed to defend their integrity, sovereignty and national resources." Thus creation of the GCC's own joint military force was "a vital necessity" aimed at defending the region against "any foreign threat."[5]

However, the exercise and its sequel, Gulf Shield II (held in Saudi Arabia in October 1984), were meant largely as a political message, at least for the near future. GCC Secretary-General Abdullah Bishara, in stressing the political rather than the military significance of the exercises, maintained that they showed the GCC countries to be serious about self-reliance, that the collective approach to defense was credible, and that a threat to one would be regarded as a threat to all. However, by late summer of 1985 the GCC had announced that no military exercises involving all its member states would be held that year. Instead, throughout 1985 a number of bilateral maneuvers involving various military services were carried out.[6] For the foreseeable future the UAE and its GCC partners will inevitably remain overwhelmingly dependent on the United States and Western Europe for modern weapons and will continue to rely heavily on those countries for operation and maintenance of sophisticated systems.

Moreover, they will require supplementary manpower, indefinitely, mostly from other Arab and Muslim countries. Finally, should a real military threat to the Gulf materialize, the U.S. Central Command (CENTCOM) would be looked to by all the Gulf states for rescue. Nevertheless, the GCC states have demonstrated more capacity for meaningful cooperation, both in economic and security matters, than most observers predicted. They have made clear their determination to assert control of their own destiny and to work together pragmatically toward that end. In that sense, the Islamic revolution in Iran and the Iran-Iraq war present a formidable threat and challenge to all the GCC states.

The Iran-Iraq War

Until the mid-1970s the UAE-Iraq relationship was, at best, strained. Baghdad's radical Ba'thist Arab nationalism caused it to lend support to groups such as PFLOAG that sought to overthrow the conservative Gulf Arab countries. Viewing itself as the bulwark of Arab nationalism against a tide of Iranian nationalism and European-U.S. "colonialism" in the Gulf region, Iraq aimed to assert itself as a Gulf state.[7] Thus, the UAE and its conservative neighbors feared Iraq as a politically destabilizing influence and a potential hegemonic power in the Gulf. This situation began to change in 1975 when the pragmatic Saddam Hussein, by then formally as well as actually the leader of Iraq, and the Shah of Iran signed the Algiers Agreement to settle outstanding disagreements, including definition both of their land and water (Shatt al-Arab) boundaries. Iraq thus became more of a status quo regional power, withdrawing its support from PFLOAG (already in retreat) and from Ba'thist cells that had been active in the UAE. With the exception of Oman, the conservative Gulf Arab states endorsed the Iraqi-sponsored Baghdad Accords, which opposed the Egyptian-Israeli peace treaty of March 1979 and voted Egypt out of the Arab League. Nevertheless, suspicions still linger about ultimate Iraqi aims in the Gulf, and relations between Iraq and the Gulf states are not likely to become cordial. The fall of the Shah and the Islamic revolution under Khomeini in Iran presented a shared threat to Iraq and the UAE, but, as will be seen, even the war has not produced a close alignment between them.

UAE relations with Iran under the Shah were, of course, strained as a result of his seizure of the Tunbs and Abu Musa. Nevertheless, the UAE and Iran shared broadly the economic, political, and security interests of status quo Gulf states, and lucrative trade across the Gulf helped boost the UAE's economic prosperity—and that of Dubai in particular. The UAE's rulers were unsettled by the advent of a revolutionary Islamic government under Ayatollah Ruhollah Khomeini in Iran. Not only does the revolution hold appeal for Shias on the Arab side of the Gulf, but it strikes a responsive chord as well with many devout Sunnis who are drawn to Khomeini's call to assert Islamic righteousness, norms and values against the alien way of life introduced from the West. The Ayatollah's message, by turn implicit and explicit, is to overturn the "corrupt regimes," which have, in his view, forsaken Islamic values, and establish virtuous Islamic governments. The success of his followers in overturning the U.S.-backed Shah provides both inspiration and a model to Shia and Sunni Muslims alike.

At the same time, it should be stressed that the tens of thousands of Iranians in the UAE have not generated any real security threat. Many are Sunni Baluchis, not enamored of either the present Iranian government nor that of the Shah. Many are conservative merchants, resident in the UAE for many years and lacking any disposition to challenge the status quo. However, the Iran-Iraq war and the several kinds of dangers it poses have created a deep dilemma and serious anxiety during the five years that the fighting has continued.

At the outbreak of the war, and since, the UAE has had little alternative but to provide diplomatic and financial support to Iraq, though professing neutrality. However, its share of the perhaps $40–50 billion of Gulf Arab financial assistance to Baghdad has been dwarfed by the contributions of the other two donors, Saudi Arabia and Kuwait. The UAE has kept a low profile, maintained a low-key dialogue with Iran, and, through Dubai and Sharjah, transshipped much-needed commodities across the Gulf. Indeed, high-level Iranian officials have on several occasions praised the UAE for the kind of good neighborly relations that others should follow with Iran.[8] Moreover, under GCC auspices and in tandem with Kuwait, the UAE has tried to play a role as mediator in the conflict.

In the spring of 1983 the foreign ministers of the UAE and Kuwait undertook a mediatory mission that apparently made some progress. Iran appeared to soften its demands for the punishment of Iraq leader Saddam Hussein and to modify its insistence on reparations from Iraq, agreeing to accept funds from the GCC states. However, the mediation effort collapsed when it was leaked prematurely.[9] Since then mediation has had little success, though officials from Iran and the GCC exchange visits. Iran's diplomatic efforts are presumably intended to cause the UAE and the other GCC states to distance themselves from Iraq.

Indeed, Iraq has been displeased with the UAE's failure to provide it greater support (i.e., diplomatic and political support) and regards the economic and communications links between the UAE and Iran as "disgraceful." The UAE's position between the war's adversaries has been described thus: "We stand with the Arabs, but this does not meant that we want to commit suicide."[10] Despite the tensions inherent in such a position, it has thus far served the UAE well and will undoubtedly persist as long as the Iran-Iraq war drags on.

After five years, the threat of spillover from the conflict is regarded with less fear than at the beginning, though the extreme vulnerability of the Gulf states to various kinds of attack on oil facilities, especially those offshore, and desalting units is a constant reminder of real danger. In 1983 and 1984 the tanker war (in which Iraq and Iran sank third-party tankers) represented a dramatic spillover of the war into the Gulf, but did not have a direct impact on the littoral states. The possibility that Iran might lash out in frustration at Iraq's supporters (because of its failure to gain military goals) via the use of fairly accurate surface-to-surface missiles constitutes some threat to the UAE.[11] However, Iran's dwindling air power and the diplomatic and commercial relationship sustained by the UAE with Iran are likely to be proof against that form of threat. Subversion continues to be regarded as a serious problem, however, with frequent reports of the apprehension of Iranian "infiltrators" (virtually all of whom are almost certainly illegal workers trying to slip into the UAE in order to get jobs rather than political plotters). Sabotage and terrorist attacks are likely to emerge as a more frequent threat.

There has been a series of apparently related terrorist incidents carried out by Shia extremists, almost certainly with ties to Iran (though evidence of the connections is almost always scanty and murky). In December 1983 several targets in Kuwait, including the French and U.S. embassies, were car-bombed. A year later members of the Shia fundamentalist underground hijacked a Kuwaiti airliner to Iran and killed two U.S. citizens in a vain attempt to force release of those who had been rounded up, tried, and imprisoned following the 1983 bombings. In mid-May 1985 a mysterious bombing occurred in Saudi Arabia, and a few days later, on May 25, the Emir of Kuwait narrowly escaped death in a suicide bombing for which the Shia Islamic Jihad claimed credit. This source of danger could grow throughout the Gulf if Iran's continued failure to press its offensive into Iraq should strengthen the hand of that faction of the Iranian leadership that favors such a strategy. However, in spite of remaining dangers, the UAE could reasonably assume that its distance from the war front combined with its own protective actions would continue to insulate it from the conflict. The outcome that the UAE would like to see is a negotiated peace that leaves neither Iran nor Iraq in a dominant position.

RELATIONS WITH THE WIDER ARAB WORLD

The UAE moved quickly after independence to pursue an active Arab policy through relations in the Arab world and participation in the Arab League. Shaikh Zayed devotes considerable time and energy to maintaining contacts with other Arab leaders and promoting inter-Arab relations. Although the UAE aims to maintain good relations with all brother Arab countries, closest and warmest ties are enjoyed with other moderate states. That is especially the case with Jordan, which has provided the UAE, together with other Gulf states, with military and security personnel who have played an important role in strengthening both defense and internal security forces. Jordan is also valued as a source of skilled and reliable labor. In return, the UAE accords Jordan diplomatic support in Arab affairs and has given it financial support (as one of the "confrontation states"—those states bordering Israel that are still technically in confrontation with it— in the Arab-Israeli conflict). When Jordan restored diplomatic relations with Egypt in 1984 the UAE did not criticize that move, although it represented a break in Arab ranks.

Relations with Egypt have been a painful problem for the UAE since Camp David. It will be recalled that, well before independence, Egypt had established links to the emirates, sustained through the years by the flow of Egyptian skills in the form of educators, office workers, and government employees. Under Anwar Sadat this became especially close and important in the military-strategic area, among others. In 1975 the Arab Military Industries Organization was established, matching Gulf money with Egyptian skills to produce weapons for its members—Egypt, Saudi Arabia, Qatar, and the UAE. Camp David abruptly ended this and led to a break in diplomatic relations between the UAE and Egypt (as well as a break in Egypt's relations with all the other Arab states except Sudan, Oman, and Somalia) and to a general loosening of economic, cultural, and other ties. The general mood in the UAE was expressed on the second anniversary of the Egyptian-Israeli peace treaty in *Al-Ittihad*, the newspaper closest to the federal government position, thus: "The example of this mishap will never lose its impact, its mark upon us as something ominous or treacherous." Yet, a year and a half later, a conservative paper in the UAE was urging reconciliation with Egypt. Moreover, to some degree at least, a modicum of military cooperation was restored between the two countries.[12] As the above-cited reaction to Jordan's reestablishment of diplomatic relations with Egypt suggests, the UAE, although unlikely to go so far itself, except in concert with several other states, has moved back toward a closer relationship with Egypt. This is likely to continue under the leadership of President Hosni Mubarak of Egypt, who has promoted Egyptian reconciliation with the Arab world. Such a reconciliation is made more urgent by the continuation of the Iran-Iraq war and the radical threats that the moderate Arab countries face in common.

UAE relations with such other moderate Arab states as Sudan and Tunisia tend to be close and friendly. Ties with Morocco are further reinforced by that nation's shared hereditary form of government. Relations with Algeria, as symbolized in the role played by Algerian experts in running the Abu Dhabi National Oil Company, have been friendly. As Algeria has increasingly moved away from its earlier radicalism, the relationship has become closer.

The UAE's relations with the radical Arab states have been wary, as was seen in the case of the PDRY. Syria has been accorded diplomatic and financial support (though the latter may now have ceased) in acknowledgment of its role in the Arab-Israeli conflict, but also because it is feared politically. The UAE and the other GCC states are, of course, unhappy about Syria's support of Iran (though the limited nature of that support is realized and the existence of a powerful countervailing rival to Iraq in the longer run is welcome). On occasion, evidence surfaces of UAE distress about Syrian policies and its desire to nudge them in a more moderate direction.[13] Libya exercises far less weight in Arab politics but is feared as a loose cannon under Muammar Qaddafi. (I happened to arrive in Abu Dhabi the same day as Qaddafi in 1981 when, following the U.S. downing of two Libyan aircraft over the Gulf of Sirte, the Libyan leader was obtaining declarations of solidarity and support from other Arab leaders. On the next day a UAE official pointedly asked why the United States insisted on undertaking actions that enhanced Qadaffi's Arab stature and forced the moderates to rally to him.)

The Arab-Israeli Conflict

Although the Iran-Iraq war and its continuing potential for spillover into the Gulf remains the current leading source of danger, the Arab-Israeli conflict is perceived as the greatest long-term threat to the stability of the Gulf Arab states, including the UAE. Until the fourth Arab-Israeli war in October 1973 and the oil embargo that grew out of it, the Arab-Israeli problem and the problems of the Gulf were generally insulated from each other, a situation from which U.S. policy consciously benefited, if it did not actually help to create it. However, by the end of the 1970s the Arab states of the Gulf—and Iran—were "emotionally, politically, and financially involved in the Arab-Israeli issue."[14] Continuation of the Arab-Israeli conflict generally abets those radical forces, including militant Islam, that threaten to undermine the stability of the UAE and the other conservative Gulf Arab countries. The large population of Palestinians and other Arabs in the UAE could compel UAE leaders to take some fairly drastic, supportive action in the event of another Arab-Israeli military round. Moreover, following the June 1981 Israeli attack on Iraq's nuclear reactor at Tuwaitha and threats by Israeli hard liners about bombing Gulf oil facilities in the event of another war, the fear of direct attack has been added to that of political instability.

The UAE, together with its Gulf neighbors, would like to see a negotiated settlement of the Arab-Israeli conflict, based on U.N. Resolutions 242 and 348 and acknowledging the right of the Palestinians to self-determination. With the exception of Oman, these countries opposed the Egyptian-Israeli peace treaty because it broke the solidarity of Arab ranks and, as we have seen, left the conservative and moderate states more vulnerable to Arab radicalism. Similarly, the GCC states, after some initial hesitation, opposed the 1983 U.S.-arranged Israeli-Lebanese withdrawal agreement because it approximated another bilateral peace agreement. GCC reaction to the September 1982 Reagan Plan has been somewhat ambivalent; although the plan holds some promise of a negotiated settlement, it stops short of providing for full Palestinian self-determination because the possibility of an independent Palestinian state is excluded.

Like other Arab states, the UAE's attitude toward the Palestinians is a mix of sympathy for brother Arabs who have suffered an injustice and annoyance and fear about hosting stateless Palestinians whose anger and frustration pose a potential security threat. As the Arab-Israeli conflict drags on, the UAE and the other Gulf states are discomfited by the lack of movement toward a solution, which allows the Palestinian problem to worsen. Moreover, with the exacerbation of the splits in the Palestinian movement following the 1982 Israeli invasion of Lebanon, an immediate practical security consideration has arisen. The Gulf states have maintained close ties with the mainstream Arafat loyalists in the Palestinian movement. It is to them that financial support has been channeled and from them that protection against extremist groups is secured. That arrangement may now be compromised because the Palestinian movement is now more fractured, and Arafat exercises less control over it.

TIES WITH OTHER THIRD WORLD COUNTRIES

The UAE plays an important role, as noted in Chapter 4, in extending significant aid to various non-Arab Third World countries, especially those within the Islamic sphere. Ties to Pakistan are close and diverse, encompassing significant aid, massive labor migration to the UAE, and important security enhancement for the UAE in the form of Pakistani officers on temporary service with the UAE's armed forces. There are important personal ties, as well, and Shaikh Zayed makes frequent visits to Pakistan. Given the number of Indian emigrant workers in the UAE, relations with the other major subcontinent state are obviously important. In general, there is significant concern in the UAE for the situation of other Muslim peoples around the world and an attempt to render assistance, sometimes in forms other than financial. For example, there have been reports of weapons, as well as money, being transferred from the UAE to the Afghan resistance fighters.[15]

The UAE and Turkey have contemplated expanded relations in response to Turkey's recent move to strengthen its links generally with the Arab world and especially to expand its economic and other ties with the Gulf Arab states. In February 1985 an agreement was drawn up to promote cooperation in trade, investment, and tourism. The possibility of creating a joint Turkish-UAE investment company and UAE investment in Turkish projects has been explored, as has been a proposal for Turkish training of UAE cadres in various fields.[16]

RELATIONS WITH WESTERN EUROPE AND JAPAN

The UAE's relations with Great Britain remain quite close, though the advantages earlier enjoyed by the British have eroded in the years since independence was achieved. The relationship is still important in economic and security terms: Britain is a major trading partner and source of weapons. British personnel still play a significant, though reduced, role in the armed forces and, in Dubai, with the internal security service. The French and, to some extent, the Italians have become additional sources of modern weapons systems as part of the UAE's effort to diversify its sources of weaponry as relations with the United States grew more strained. There has been some criticism of France for its more pro-Israel stance under President François Mitterrand than was the case under Valéry Giscard d'Estaing. That country, however, has become the UAE's principal source of military aircraft, and its Mirage-2000 has been selected as the backbone of the UAE's air force.

With the other GCC countries, the UAE has looked to the EEC to provide some initiative in promoting an Arab-Israeli settlement. The Gulf states have grown increasingly unhappy about what they see as declining U.S. effort and credibility in that regard. However, beyond the Venice Declaration of 1980, which called for an evenhanded approach in the peace process, and a few subsequent diplomatic initiatives, this strategy has accomplished relatively little. The UAE and its neighbors recognize that Europe cannot, on its own without the United States, promote the peace process any more than it can defend them against possible hostile actions by the Soviets, unless there is U.S. involvement. Yet the European connection not only offers tangible benefits to the GCC but generates a dialogue on political and other issues that could have long-term benefits. If the EEC and GCC can come to agreement on an economic cooperation pact, overcoming points of contention, especially on the sale of Gulf petrochemicals in Europe, the links between the two groupings of countries could grow significantly.

Japan, as was seen in Chapter 4, has become an important UAE trading partner and source of advanced civilian technology. The relationship goes very little beyond the economic realm. It is political only to the extent that the Japanese occasionally feel the need to make public statements calling for an evenhanded approach to the Arab-Israeli problem. In an indirect way, Japan has attempted to play a diplomatic role of potentially great importance to the UAE and the other Gulf states by mediating the Iran-Iraq war because it is an important economic partner of each belligerent. However, these efforts have not yielded fruit, and like others of a similar nature, are unlikely to do so because Iran will not settle the war peacefully as long as Saddam Hussein is in power in Iraq.

RELATIONS WITH THE SOVIETS, THE EASTERN BLOC, AND THE PEOPLE'S REPUBLIC OF CHINA

The communist world has assumed a much less significant place in the UAE's pattern of interests and relationships than have Western Europe and the United States. Although the Gulf states generally (Oman excepted) have not perceived a Soviet threat to the Gulf in the immediate or largely military terms that the United States has, they are concerned about Soviet intentions, especially after the 1979 invasion of Afghanistan. Essentially pragmatic considerations are likely to determine their relationships with the Soviet bloc, but the professed atheism of communist leaders does color the Gulf states' perceptions and relations with the USSR negatively. The UAE, however, has seen various Soviet statements and actions on the Arab-Israeli issue and the Palestinian question in a positive light. As it has grown more disenchanted with the United States, the UAE looks to the Soviets to some extent to promote diplomatic movement toward a settlement. Although the UAE is prepared to accord more diplomatic weight to the Soviets on Gulf issues to help guard against superpower rivalry there, it opposed (with all the other GCC states except Kuwait) the Brezhnev Gulf security initiative that would have given the USSR more of a voice in Gulf affairs than the states of the area could accept.[17]

In recent years the USSR has generally adopted a more moderate approach to the Gulf area, loosening its ties to radical groups there and helping to achieve some modest diplomatic and commercial breakthroughs. It is likely that, for some time at least, the Soviets will seek to extend and exploit these kinds of gains, rather than embark on an adventurous military course. Thus, in the early 1980s the Soviets and several Eastern Bloc countries have begun to develop new ties with the UAE, including commercial air links, establishment of trade offices, and exchange of official visits. In early 1985 the USSR and Poland offered scholarships for study by UAE students in both countries in a number of fields including communications, physics, and history.[18] It was not immediately apparent if any of these scholarships might be used. However, in November 1985, as we have seen, formal diplomatic ties were established with the Soviet Union. The Saudis, too, have increased their own indirect and informal ties with the Soviets. Saudi Arabia has from time to time hinted at establishing formal relations with Moscow as the UAE has done. One consideration that probably causes hesitation is the fear of the political activities and influence that might follow as a consequence of a Soviet and Eastern Bloc diplomatic presence.

There has been speculation that the long-anticipated decline in Soviet oil production, begun in the mid-1980s, would force Soviet dependence on Gulf oil and perhaps even compel a forceful Soviet move into the Gulf. However, the Soviets possess vast gas and coal reserves that can be drawn on as oil grows less plentiful. Depending on their prevailing energy mix and balance of requirements for domestic use and export of energy, the Soviets might seek to purchase oil from Gulf sources. Soviet purchase of a fairly considerable amount of oil from Saudi Arabia in 1983 drew attention, but was presumably taken in payment for Soviet arms shipments to Iraq.[19]

In 1984 the UAE extended diplomatic recognition to the People's Republic of China (PRC). This may, in part, reflect the modest economic relationship that has developed with the PRC. In February 1985 a PRC delegation visited the UAE to promote cooperation in the field of urban and rural construction. Whether the establishment of formal ties with the PRC is meant to be a prelude to such relations with Eastern Bloc countries as well as the Soviets remained uncertain as of late 1985.

THE UNITED STATES AND THE UAE: A MIXED RELATIONSHIP

As we have seen (in Chapter 4), the United States has important economic relations with the UAE. The UAE looks to the United States as a prime source of current technology and (with some reservation) for external security assistance. However, the political relationship between the two nations is strained, and the credibility of U.S. support and friendship has suffered in recent years.

Recent U.S. policy failures have tended to shake the UAE's confidence in U.S. pledges of support. Most unsettling, of course, was the fall of the Shah, which occurred despite his long and close alignment with the United States. U.S. inability to resolve the Iranian hostage crisis (1979–1981) for more than a year left an image of U.S. impotency even as the possibility that the United States might resort to precipitate use of force, out of frustration, generated considerable worry about Soviet and other reactions to such a move. Moreover, the U.S. response to the Soviet invasion of Afghanistan—creation of the Rapid Deployment Force (now CENTCOM)—raised perhaps as many fears as it alleviated. Like many small states offered the protection of great powers, and with fresh memories of then Secretary of State Henry Kissinger's threat to seize Gulf oil fields, the UAE and its neighbors were led to wonder *"Sed quis custodiet ipsos custodes?"* (But who is to guard the guardians themselves?).

The Arab-Israeli conflict has generated the greatest strains in the U.S.-UAE relationship. Disagreement between the two nations is not entirely a matter of principle (in the abstract, at least, the United States and UAE are not far apart on the appropriate terms for a settlement); the UAE views U.S. actions (or inaction) as dangerous to UAE security and indicative of a lack of concern for the UAE's well-being. The level of U.S. economic and military support for Israel, the failure (in UAE and other Arab eyes) of the United States to restrain Israeli "agressions" such as the 1978 incursion and 1981 air strike against Lebanon and the 1981 bombing of Iraq's nuclear reactor, the persistent U.S. vetoes of U.N. Security Council resolutions against Israeli actions on the West Bank, and the green light believed to have been given by Washington for Israel's 1982 invasion of Lebanon— all these and other actions have persuaded the UAE that the United States is almost totally one-sided in its approach to the Middle East's dominating issue. As one UAE official has stated it, the United States, in the UAE's view, appears to believe that it can support Israeli dominance in the region and simultaneously pursue friendly and productive relations with the Arabs while keeping the Soviets out of the Middle East.[20] The leaders of the UAE believe that the Arab side has, through the Fez plan adopted at the 1982 Arab League summit and the efforts of King Hussein bin Talal of Jordan and PLO leader Yasser Arafat to find a negotiating formula to advance peace, conformed to the "fair and reasonable compromises" that President Reagan's September 1982 peace initiative called for. However, perceived U.S. failure to pursue vigorously an approach to a negotiated peace on the basis of its own stated principles is, in UAE eyes, cause for doubting the credibility of U.S. commitments. Thus, the UAE's relationship with the United States is a liability with respect to the dangers to UAE stability and security that are inherent in the Arab-Israeli conflict. For that reason, the UAE has, for the past several years, been distancing itself politically from the United States.

This distancing, evident in UAE criticism of U.S. policy in the Gulf as well as on the Arab-Israeli conflict, has led the UAE to a more neutralist stance and a reluctance, publicly at least, to be seen cooperating closely with the United States in political or security matters. A certain compartmentalizing in the relationship has made possible the maintenance of strong, mutually beneficial economic ties while it becomes more difficult for the United States and the UAE to work together in other areas. The UAE still wishes to acquire U.S. weapons such as Hawk air defense missiles and has reportedly been interested in purchasing F-16 fighting aircraft. Moreover, the United States remains the over-the-horizon protector that would be called on if an overwhelming external threat to the UAE should occur. However, the strains in the relationship have helped lead to major weapons systems purchases outside the United States, thereby reducing the capacity for UAE cooperation in air defenses with U.S.-supplied Saudi Arabia. Additionally, the diminished quantity and quality of UAE consultation on defense issues with the United States may compromise the military coordination that would be required to respond effectively to a potential external security crisis.[21]

Fears of spillover from the Iran-Iraq war have compelled closer security relations for the UAE and the other GCC countries with the United States than would otherwise have existed during the past few years. If, as appears to be the case in mid-1985, the war's large-scale military actions are winding down, a greater danger will reside in the possibility of subversion and terrorist sabotage operations launched by Iran or carried out by Arab Shia extremists with Iranian encouragement and/or support. Together with these, the ideological appeal of militant revolutionary Islam will constitute the greatest immediate threat to the UAE. The United States can do little to assist in countering these dangers; indeed, regarding the last, the United States is a part of the problem, not part of the solution. Although the tide of revolutionary Islam of the sort espoused in Iran will begin to ebb (though the essential strength of Islam in both private and public spheres will remain), close alignment between the UAE and the United States will not be sought. The prospects are that the relationship will remain strained.

SECURITY PROSPECTS

The UAE has demonstrated a considerable capacity for surviving the various external threats that have challenged its security since independence. Its astute diplomacy in the face of the current threat of revolutionary Iran and its role in the Gulf Cooperation Council in advancing cooperation on security as well as economic goals help to protect the UAE against regional dangers. In the near term, at least, a major military threat, either from across the Gulf or from more distant sources, seems unlikely. Although subversion and terrorism are greater possibilities, the UAE seems to have guarded reasonably well against these dangers with a judicious mix of diplomatic and social policies and internal security (though the latter needs to be improved). Perhaps the primary challenge the UAE faces at the moment is how to balance its considerable security reliance and dependence for trade and technology on the West, and especially the United States, with the need to accommodate the threat represented by the ideological appeal of resurgent Islam.

Future uncertainties loom in the Gulf and the wider Middle East. The most likely outcome of the Iran-Iraq war would appear to be a kind of standoff, with victory denied to either side. The combatants' exhaustion and urgent need for reconstruction following the bloody and destructive conflict are likely to prevent them from immediately pursuing a forward policy in the Gulf. However, as was suggested above, the frustration of some of the more extreme factions in Iran could induce them to promote wide-scale subversion and terrorism against the Gulf Arab states. Eventually, it is almost certain that both Iran and Iraq will seek to play a dominating role in the Gulf. The UAE and its GCC partners may face Iraqi (possibly also Iranian) demands for a role in that organization. How long and effectively the moderate Arab alignment engendered by the Iran-Iraq war to guard against the Iranian threat will last is also another source of uncertainty whose implications are far from positive. If the perceived threat should diminish sufficiently, that alignment would be likely to weaken, perhaps compromising Egypt's reintegration in the Arab fold and generally exposing the UAE and its conservative neighbors to the currents of Middle Eastern radicalism, from right to left.

Several other trends and developments may coincide so as to add to the potential security dangers and challenges of the next decade or so. Domestic U.S. oil reserves are rapidly declining as are those of most non-OPEC exporters, and explorations outside the Middle East have generally been very disappointing. This suggests that by the mid-1990s an OPEC sellers' market is likely to have been reestablished with its center of gravity in the Gulf. The UAE and its neighbors might then come under radical Arab pressure once again to use oil as a weapon to force a settlement of the Arab-Israeli issue. Moreover, by then the UAE will be under the leadership of another generation, adding further to the uncertainty of its capacity to cope with new challenges. Before such a situation comes to pass, the UAE will have faced another consitutional crisis in 1986, upon whose resolution much will depend. However, if the past is indeed prologue, the UAE's future prospects, for at least the next several years, must be judged reasonably good.

NOTES

1. Brian Fredericks, "The Gulf Cooperation Council at the Two Year Mark" (May 16, 1983), unpublished paper, pp. 5, 6.

2. Anthony H. Cordesman, *The Gulf and the Search for Strategic Stability: Saudi Arabia, the Military Balance in the Gulf, and Trends in the Arab-Israeli Military Balance* (Boulder, Colo.: Westview Press, 1984), p. 597.

3. Thomas L. McNaugher, *Arms and Oil: U.S. Military Strategy and the Persian Gulf* (Washington, D.C.: The Brookings Institution, 1985), p. 216.

4. Cordesman, *The Gulf and the Search for Strategic Stability*, pp. 600–601.

5. Raghida Dergham, "The GCC Is Now a Reality," *The Middle East*, no. 109 (November 1983):16.

6. Raghida Dergham, "We Don't Need Volunteers to Protect Our House," interview with Abdullah Bishara, *The Middle East,* no. 109 (November 1983):16; "GCC: No 'Peninsula Shield Exercises in 1985,'" *Al-Ittihad* (Abu Dhabi) (in Arabic), September 9, 1985, in Foreign Broadcast Information Service (hereafter referred to as FBIS), *Daily Report: Middle East and Africa* 5, no. 176 (September 11, 1985):C3.

7. Jasim M. Abdulghani, *Iraq and Iran: The Years of Crisis* (Baltimore, Md.: Johns Hopkins University Press, 1984), pp. 78–79.

8. See, for example, the statement of President Ali Khamene'i cited in "IRNA: Deputy Prime Minister Hands Message to President," IRNA (Iran News Agency, Tehran) (in English), September 17, 1984, in FBIS, *Daily Report: Middle East and Africa* 5, no. 182 (September 17, 1984):C3.

9. See "Iran Foreign Ministry Official Arrives on Visit," WAKH (Gulf News Agency, Manama, Bahrain) (in Arabic), May 31, 1983, and "Meets with Government Officials" from same source, June 1, 1983, in FBIS, *Daily Report: Middle East and Africa* 5, no. 106 (June 1, 1983):C3; David B. Ottaway, "Iran Accepts Gulf State Mediation in War with Iraq," *Washington Post,* May 21, 1983, p. A18; and Chris Kutschera, "A War That Fuels Gulf Fears," *The Middle East,* no. 127 (May 1985):18.

10. Kutschera, "A War That Fuels Gulf Fears," p. 18.

11. See Middle East Assessment Group, "Missiles in the Gulf: Missiles in the Third World," Bulletin no. 13 (Washington, D.C.: MEAG, May 1985), p. 2.

12. *Al-Ittihad* (in Arabic), March 25, 1981, p. 1; and "Emirates Delegation Arrives in Egypt," UPI dispatch in *Washington Post,* December 5, 1982, p. A31.

13. See, for example, "Reports on Offering Syria Oil Denied," WAKH (Manama) (in Arabic), July 6, 1984, in FBIS, *Daily Report: Middle East and Africa* 5, no. 131 (July 6, 1984):C2. A UAE official was cited as denying reports that the UAE had offered Syria oil if the latter would "review some of its international stands."

14. Hermann Frederick Eilts, "Security Considerations in the Persian Gulf," *International Security* 5, no. 2 (Fall 1980):85.

15. See William Branigin, "Feuding Guerilla Groups Rely on Uneasy Pakistan," *Washington Post,* October 22, 1983, p. A10.

16. See the following reports: "UAE President Interviewed on Gulf Issues," WAKH (Manama) (in Arabic), February 21, 1985, in FBIS, *Daily Report: Middle East and Africa* 5, no. 36 (February 22, 1985):C5; and "PRC Construction, Environmental Minister Arrives," WAKH (Manama) (in Arabic), February 26, 1985, in FBIS, *Daily Report: Middle East and Africa* 5, no. 39 (February 27, 1985):C3.

17. Nadia Hijab, "Gulf Peace Seekers: Patching Up Arab Quarrels," *The Middle East,* no. 170 (December 1983):15; and Dimitri K. Simes, "Soviet Strategy on Syria and the Persian Gulf," Executive Report no. 3 (Washington, D.C.: Middle East Institute, August 13, 1984), p. 7.

18. See the following reports: "Zayid Receives Cable from Poland's Jablonski," WAM (Abu Dhabi) (in Arabic), August 5, 1984, in FBIS, *Daily*

Report: Middle East and Africa 5, no. 152 (August 6, 1984):C6; "Official Returns from Moscow Meeting," *Khaleej Times* (Dubai) (in English), September 3, 1984, in FBIS, *Daily Report: Middle East and Africa* 5, no. 172 (September 4, 1984):C5; "WAKH: USSR Offers Scholarships to UAE Students," WAKH (Manama) (in Arabic), January 21, 1985, in FBIS, *Daily Report: Middle East and Africa* 5, no. 15 (January 23, 1985):C6; and "Poland Offers Postgraduate Scholarships," *Al-Khalij* (Sharjah) (in Arabic), January 25, 1985, in FBIS, *Daily Report: Middle East and Africa* 5, no. 16 (January 24, 1985):C5–C6.

19. Simes, "Soviet Strategy," p. 9.

20. Ghanim Faris Al-Mazrui, "U.S.-Gulf Arab Economic Relations," *American-Arab Affairs*, no. 4 (Spring 1983):80.

21. "Rumors of Providing Facilities to U.S. RDF Denied," WAKH (Manama) (in Arabic), April 25, 1985, in FBIS, *Daily Report: Middle East and Africa* 5, no. 80 (April 25, 1985):C5.

Acronyms and Abbreviations

AC&W	air control and warning
ADCO	Abu Dhabi Company for Onshore Oil Operations
ADFAED	Abu Dhabi Fund for Arab Economic Development
ADMA-Opco	Abu Dhabi Marine Areas Operating Company
ADNOC	Abu Dhabi National Oil Company
AIOC	Anglo-Iranian Oil Company
Aramco	Arabian American Oil Company
AWACS	Air Warning and Command System
bpd	barrels per day
CASOC	California Arabian Standard Oil Company
CENTCOM	U.S. Central Command
C^3I	command, control, communications, and intelligence
DUBAL	Dubai Aluminum Company
DUCAL	Dubai Cables
DUGAS	Dubai Gas Company
EEC	European Economic Community
FAO	Food and Agriculture Organization
FNC	Federal National Council
GCC	Gulf Cooperation Council
IPC	Iraq Petroleum Company
LNG	liquified natural gas
LPG	liquified petroleum gas
mbpd	million barrels per day
NBAD	National Bank of Abu Dhabi
OAPEC	Organization of Arab Petroleum Exporting Countries
OPEC	Organization of Petroleum Exporting Countries
PDRY	People's Democratic Republic of Yemen
PD(TC)	Petroleum Development (Trucial Coast)

PFLO	Popular Front for the Liberation of Oman
PFLOAG	Popular Front for the Liberation of the Occupied Arab Gulf
PLO	Palestine Liberation Organization
PRC	People's Republic of China
SFC	Supreme Federal Council
SHEDCO	Sharjah Economic Development Corporation
TOL	Trucial Oman Levies
TOS	Trucial Oman Scouts
UAE	United Arab Emirates
UBME	Union Bank of the Middle East
USDA	United States Department of Agriculture
WAM	Wikalat Anba al-Imarat

Suggestions for Further Reading

CHAPTER 1: LAND AND PEOPLE

The literature available on the United Arab Emirates in general is not extensive, and on the geography and demography of the UAE and the whole of the lower Gulf it is particulary scanty. There is useful material in *The Persian Gulf States: A General Survey*, edited by Alvin J. Cottrell et al. (Baltimore and London: Johns Hopkins University Press, 1980), especially in some of the appendixes. K. G. Fenelon's *The United Arab Emirates: An Economic and Social Survey*, 2nd ed. (London and New York: Longman, 1976) and Donald Hawley's *The Trucial States* (London: George Allen and Unwin, Ltd., 1971) also provide helpful information—again mainly in their appendixes. Michael Tomkinson's *The United Arab Emirates: An Insight and a Guide* (London: Michael Tomkinson Publishing, 1975) is a good, though somewhat dated, introduction to the country. It includes well-written descriptions of the various regions of the UAE with numerous photographs that help to convey a sense of the land. Frauke Heard-Bey's *From Trucial States to United Arab Emirates* (London and New York: Longman, 1982), a compendious source generally on the UAE, may be usefully consulted. J. G. Lorimer's classic *Gazetteer of the Persian Gulf, Oman and Central Arabia* (Calcutta: Superintendent Government Printing, 1915), first issued between 1908 and 1915, remains a rich source as does S. B. Miles's *The Countries and Tribes of the Persian Gulf* (London: Harrison and Sons, 1919).

CHAPTER 2: THE HISTORICAL BACKGROUND

On the ancient past of the UAE and the lower Gulf area the first book to turn to is Geoffrey Bibby's *Looking for Dilmun* (Harmondsworth, England: Penguin Books, 1980), which describes the dramatic archeological findings of the 1950s and 1960s. Tomkinson, in the book cited above, provides some interesting information on discoveries made in various digs up to the mid-1970s in the UAE. In *The Middle East* (London) and other periodicals fragments of the fascinating, ongoing rediscovery of the earliest history of this area are revealed from time to time. The two chapters by Roger M. Savory in the book edited by Cottrell and noted above provide a good, brief introduction to the ancient and early modern periods of Gulf history. George Hourani in *Arab Seafaring in the Indian Ocean in Ancient and Early Medieval Times* (Princeton, N.J.: Princeton University Press, 1956) tells of the long domination of Indian Ocean trade by Arab merchants and sailors. Allan Villiers, in *Sons of Sinbad* (New York: Charles Scribner's Sons, 1940), and Tim Severin, in *The Sindbad Voyage* (New York: C. P. Putnam's Sons, 1983), write interestingly of latter-day, firsthand adventures illuminating the accomplishments of early Arab mariners. Malcolm Yapp's two extended essays in the Cottrell volume offer a good introduction to the history of the Gulf in the modern era and provide a useful description and analysis of the British trucial system. The classic study of the latter subject is J. B. Kelly's *Britain and the Persian Gulf* (London: Oxford University Press, 1968). The same author's *Eastern Arabian Frontiers* (New York and London: Frederick A. Praeger, 1964) contains useful background to the Saudi Arabia–Abu Dhabi border dispute, though it is marked by anti-Saudi and anti-U.S. bias. His *Arabia, the Gulf & the West: A Critical View of the Arabs and Their Oil Policy* (New York: Basic Books, 1980) is a provocative exegesis on the British withdrawal from the Gulf and its consequences that is marred by splenetically vented prejudices.

On the twentieth-century background several recent books are informative. The director of the Center for Documentation and Research in Abu Dhabi, Muhammad Morsy Abdullah, has written *The United Arab Emirates: A Modern History* (London and New York: Croom Helm and Barnes and Noble, 1978). Frauke Heard-Bey's *From Trucial States to United Arab Emirates* includes useful information on the modern historical background, with an especially interesting chapter devoted to the development of Dubai in the twentieth century. Rosemarie Said Zahlan's *The Origins of the United Arab Emirates: A Political and Social Study of the Trucial States* (New York: St. Martin's Press, 1978) is a detailed history of the period between the world wars.

CHAPTER 3: SOCIETY AND CULTURE

Readers unfamiliar with the Islamic world may wish to pursue further a general understanding of Islam and its impact on social and political life in the Middle East and beyond. Of the many excellent books to appear on the subject in recent years two, in particular, are recommended: John Esposito, *Islam and Politics* (Syracuse, N.Y.: Syracuse University Press, 1984), and Malise Ruthven, *Islam in the World* (New York and Oxford: Oxford University Press, 1984). Frauke Heard-Bey's previously cited work contains a wealth of information on traditional social structure and dynamics, with a lengthy section on many aspects of tribal society. The chapter by Ralph Magnus, "Societies and Social Change in the Persian Gulf," in the Cottrell volume cited above, provides a good analysis of the sources of cohesion in traditional Gulf society and the challenge of change to the conservative sociocultural norms of the UAE and its neighbors. In *Arabia: A Journey Through the Labyrinth* (New York: Simon and Schuster, 1979), the British journalist Jonathan Raban offers insights into the process of change in the UAE, how it is psychologically accommodated, and the price it exacts. Linda Usru Soffan's *The Women of the United Arab Emirates* (London and New York: Croom Helm and Barnes and Noble, 1980) is a pioneering study that outlines the impact of change on UAE women and suggests some of the ways in which traditional male-female relationships are being altered. In a fascinating, specialized study, *Aesthetics and Ritual in the United Arab Emirates* (Beirut: American University of Beirut Press, 1983), Aida S. Kanafani deals with elements of traditional behavior that are still an important part of UAE society. "Growing Up in the Gulf," the cover story in *The Middle East*'s August 1985 issue examines the impact of massive, rapid change on youth. In its "Mosaic" section that same publication frequently carries reports and analyses of social and cultural developments in the UAE and the Gulf. Access to articles on the same subjects in Arabic publications can be gained through the translations of the Joint Publications Research Service (JPRS) in Washington, D.C. Those who can read French will find an engaging personal view of the UAE in Monique Jegou's *Les Emirats Arabes Unis* (Paris: Albin Michel, 1983).

CHAPTER 4: THE ECONOMY: RUSH TO AFFLUENCE

The Frauke Heard-Bey study cited under previous chapter headings contains interesting information on the traditional economy of the UAE. In *The Economic Development of the United Arab Emirates* (New York: St. Martin's Press, 1981), Ragaei el-Mallakh provides a useful view of the modern economy. Generally, the best way to track economic developments is through serial publications of which the most helpful are the *Middle East Economic Digest* (MEED) and the *Middle East Economic Survey* (MEES), both published weekly. MEED issues special reports on individual countries; those on the UAE appear toward the end of the calendar year. It has also put out *The UAE: A MEED Practical Guide* (London: Middle East Economic Digest Ltd., 1982), edited by Trevor Mostyn, containing much useful information on the economy and other aspects of the country. *The Middle East* presents a business and finance survey in each issue including frequent reports on the UAE, among them profiles of important business figures. *Middle East Executive Reports* (Washington, D.C.) provides nuggets of current information and analysis on legal and business issues. The *Foreign Economic Trends* reports on the UAE, prepared by the Department of State and published by the Department of Commerce, are a further useful source. As handy sources of basic information the State Department's "Post Reports" are similarly helpful.

CHAPTER 5: DOMESTIC POLITICS: THE COURSE OF FEDERATION

The best guide to the dynamics of the federal and emiral politics of the UAE remains John Duke Anthony's 1975 study, *Arab States of the Lower Gulf: People Politics, Petroleum* (Washington, D.C.: The Middle East Institute, 1975), unfortunately long out of print. A valuable study of the federal experiment is Ali Mohammed Khalifa, *The United Arab Emirates: Unity in Fragmentation* (Boulder, Colo.: Westview Press, 1979). Current political developments may be followed in various periodicals and the daily press. A highly useful guide is the "Modern History and Politics" section of the quarterly *Middle East Journal*'s (Washington, D.C.) "Guide to Periodical Literature." In addition to the above-cited JPRS translations, a prime source of translated material is the Foreign Broadcast Informtion Service (FBIS), which covers the Arabian Peninsula in section C of volume 5, *Daily Report: Middle East & North Africa*.

CHAPTER 6: THE REGIONAL AND INTERNATIONAL ARENAS: SECURITY DANGERS AND PROSPECTS

Of a number of recent works dealing with security issues in the Gulf first mention should be given to Anthony H. Cordesman's compendious and thoughtful study *The Gulf and the Search for Strategic Stability: Saudi Arabia, the Military Balance in the Gulf, and Trends in the Arab-Israeli Military Balance* (Boulder, Colo.: Westview Press, 1984). The London International Institute for Strategic Studies has issued a useful set of four brief volumes under the general title *Security in the Persian Gulf* (London: IISS, Vols. 1 and 2, 1981, Vols. 3 and 4, 1982) which examines domestic, regional, and international factors. A pertinent recent study is Thomas L. McNaugher, *Arms and Oil: U.S. Military Strategy and the Persian Gulf* (Washington, D.C.: The Brookings Institution, 1985). The *Middle East Journal* should be regularly reviewed for relevant current periodical sources, and the diligent researcher will want to keep up with what is published by FBIS and *Arab Report and Record* (London). Other periodicals worth singling out for useful articles are the aforementioned *The Middle East*, together with *American-Arab Affairs, Defense and Foreign Affairs, Defense Week* (all Washington, D.C. publications), *International Security* (Cambridge, Mass.), and *Islamic World Defense* (London). Finally, the committee prints issued by the United States Congress, especially by the subcommittees of the Senate Foreign Relations Committee and the House Foreign Affairs Committee that deal with the Middle East are valuable sources of information on political and security issues in the Gulf region.

Index